T0171459

Len's Lines

A Little Religion on a Positive Note

Leonard Granger

WestBow
PRESS
A DIVISION OF THOMAS NELSON

WestBow Press books may be ordered through booksellers or by contacting:

WestBow Press
A Division of Thomas Nelson
1663 Liberty Drive
Bloomington, IN 47403
www.westbowpress.com
1-(866) 928-1240

Because of the dynamic nature of the Internet, any web addresses or links contained in this book may have changed since publication and may no longer be valid. The views expressed in this work are solely those of the author and do not necessarily reflect the views of the publisher, and the publisher hereby disclaims any responsibility for them.

Any people depicted in stock imagery provided by Thinkstock are models, and such images are being used for illustrative purposes only.

Certain stock imagery © Thinkstock.

ISBN: 978-1-4497-7657-2 (sc)

Library of Congress Control Number: 2012921934

Printed in the United States of America

WestBow Press rev. date: 11/27/2012

Introduction

This book I believe is an example of Christian living; as we put our gracious and loving Lord and Savior Jesus Christ first in our lives. Our Lord is there to carry us over the trials and tribulations of life and put us on the solid higher ground if we only put our Hope, Trust, and Faith in Him.

The short story columns that make up this book were first published in the Dixon Tribune of Dixon, California and it was through the effort of the editor and staff that the owning company agreed to publishing, "Lens Lines — A Little Religion On A Positive Note." I had been a writer of fishing reports for newspapers since 1972 and asked to change to their religious page two years ago. My purpose was to write stories on Christian Living that I prayed would get people to again return to the church of their choice and worship our Lord Jesus Christ. As I have no Bible College training it has been a challenge to write, but I ask in prayer for the Lord to guide me. I am very thankful to my Pastor Gerald Harder who reviews the columns for spiritual correctness as applied to the stories.

As an Iowan country boy who is now eighty years young and living on my farm in California, the columns have a country flavor in many cases. Trust you will enjoy how the Lord has affected my life and those that have contributed their stories to make Lens Lines—A Little Religion on a Positive Note.

Reaching Out

As I write this column each week I pray that it is reaching out to the readers with broad enough subjects that it will keep their interest. We read in the newspapers where the population of our wonderful country is turning away from the God that has blessed us over and over . Why do we think now that the government is all powerful and can take care of our needs? I try in this column to get our people back to church and put their trust in the Lord. Our founding fathers of this country looked to God and our country was founded on Biblical principles. "In God We Trust" even appears on our coins and money we circulate all over the world, but is it now only words?

People have asked why I write my column Lens Lines? I write as God has spoken to me from His Word and try to quote Bible verses in the columns. If you want to read the many columns they appear on TipTopWebsite.com/LensLines. and many go worldwide on Faithwriters.com to 190 countries.

God gave us His Book the Bible, the most read book of all time, filled with inspired verses and stories from the beginning of our earth that will guide and direct us. It covers every aspect of our lives and how men of God in the Old Testament reached out to the heavenly power for answers as they met the trials and tribulations of their time. Then in the New Testament, God sent His Son Jesus Christ to give us a way to reach His Father. In John 3-17, " For God did not send His Son into the world to condemn the world, but that the world through Him might be saved". He died on the cross and shed His blood to cover our sins, was buried and rose again on the third day. Our living gracious and loving Lord and Savior Jesus Christ now sits on the right hand of His Father in Heaven and everything we encounter today is in His plan as we put our Hope, Trust and Faith in Him.

We today have the Bible to guide and direct us as we likewise face the world with all its problems. If we only pray and read the Bible daily asking for the Lords help He will bless us as it says in the Bible. Matthew 21-22 , And "All things, whatsoever ye shall ask in prayer, believing, ye shall receive". And in John 14-6 Jesus said, " I am the way. the truth , and the life. No man cometh unto the Father but by Me." I pray our country will turn to God for answers of our pressing problems just as our founding fathers.

Trust this Sunday each of us will be in the church of our choice singing and worshiping our Lord and Savior Jesus Christ.

God Bless America

We Ask God Questions Apr 3. 2011

God gives us blessings that we often do not even see or act on. Here is something we can all rejoice with, as God answers our questions.

I Asked God

I asked God to take away my habit.

God said, "No. It is not for me to take away, but for you to give it up."

I asked God to make my handicapped child whole.

God said, "No. Your spirit is whole, your body is only temporary."

I asked God to grant me patience.

God said, "No. Patience is a by-product of tribulations; it isn't granted, it is learned."

I asked God to give me happiness.

God said, "No. I give you blessings; happiness is up to you."

I asked God to spare me pain.

God said, "No. Suffering draws you apart from worldly cares and brings you closer to me."

I asked God to make my spirit grow.

God said, "No. You must grow on your own! But I will prune you to make you fruitful."

I asked God for all things that I might enjoy life.

God said, "No. I will give you life, so that you may enjoy all things."

I asked God to help me LOVE others, as much as He loves me.

God said... "Ahhhh, finally you have the idea.

Anonymous

God Bless America

Prayer Needed Today April 8, 2011

After reading that only some three percent of the people in California are in church on any Sunday, I prayed Lord what would you like me to do??? He answered my prayers saying, use a blessing I have given you to reach out to fellow Christians, , as God is still the answer for all problems. America is a great nation but it has turned away from God, who is the provider of all things, and we have forgotten how our founders made this country great with God's help . Let us all remember to pray daily and praise the Lord for all the blessings he has given us.

Someone has said that if Christians really understood the full power we have available through prayer, we might be speechless.

Did you know that during WWII there was an advisor to Churchill who organized a group of people who dropped what they were doing every day at a prescribed hour for just one minute to collectively pray for the safety of England, its people and peace?

There is now a group of people organizing the same thing in America. If you my fellow Christians would like to participate: Evening prayer at 9:00 PM Eastern Time, 8 PM Central, 7 PM Mountain, and 6 PM Pacific, let us stop one minute and pray for the safety of the United States, our troops, our citizens, and for a return to a Godly nation. If you know anyone else who would like to join us and participate, please pass this along.

Our prayers are the most powerful asset we have; so let us pray that our fellow Dixon neighbors will put their trust in God and again fill to overflowing our churches.

God Bless America

No Regrets April 15, 2011

One day a bunch of friends about my age, including Jim a tall balding type of near 80, met for a pleasant lunch. When the menus were brought to the table they all ordered salads and sandwiches, except Jim who said, Ice Cream, please two scoops of chocolate.

The group were not sure they had heard Jim correctly when he added, along with heated apple pie. They could not take their eyes off their friend Jim as he ate his pie a-la-mode. So ended a friendly meal get together but they were confused.

A few days later my friend says he went out again with Jim as he ordered a Parfait. Jim asked my friend, "Does my ordering confuse you and my friend answered, " You sure are different than when we ate out last month— How come you order rich desserts instead of the sensible foods you used to order?

This was Jim's answer: "I try to eat the food I need and the things I should, however. life is so short, I hate missing out on something good. So before I die, I want to try all those things over the years I have ignored. —- I have not smelled all the flowers yet, fished all the trout streams, flown enough kites or enjoyed all the wonderful fudge sundaes. I still want to try out more golf courses and laugh at your jokes, wade in the water again and feel the ocean spray on my face.

I want to attend an old fashion country church, that is God fearing and preaches the old time religion from the King James original bible. Lord, I am ready to meet you whenever you decide to call me home, so I am getting ready visiting, attending, and eating all the wonderful things you have blessed us with here on earth.

I want peanut butter every day and still want un-timed phone calls to those I love. I have not cried enough at the movies or walked in enough morning rains. I want to be in love again as you Lord love me So, if I have a desert instead of having a dinner, and you call if me home before night fall, I would say I died a winner.

We all need to be reminded that: Happiness isn't based on possessions, power, or prestige—-but with people we like and respect. A LOVING RELATIONSHIP WITH ALMIGHTY GOD IS IMPORTANT....

Remember that while money talks, Chocolate Ice Cream Sings.

God Bless America

Beauty and the Beast

Some consider the fairy tale Beauty and the Beast to be the most beloved love story of all time. The foundational theme of the story has been used in many movies and books throughout the years. It is the story of a spoiled prince who snubs an old beggar woman at his castle because of her unattractive appearance.

The woman warns the prince not to make judgments by appearance. Repeatedly she returns to the castle, but each time the prince turns her away. After her final dismissal, the old woman turns into a beautiful princess. She also casts a spell on the prince that turns him into a beastly looking creature. The only way to erase the ugliness of his appearance is that he learn to love another and earn her love in return. The rest of the story is a familiar one of the triumph of love over appearance.

And it is an illustration of grace as well. How ugly we were in our sin! Our sin-marred appearance was repulsive to God. But the God of grace saw beyond the ugliness of sin and He loved the unlovely. Christians often quote that most fundamental of Bible truths from John 3:16 : For God so loved the world. . . . " Unfortunately, we don't often grasp how much love that took.

There is a twist to this story of grace that we must not overlook. The beast in the fairy tale had to learn to express love to win the beauty to himself. God, on the other hand, was the Beautiful One who made the first step by expressing love to ugly and sinful humanity by giving

His Son for us. Paul puts it this way: "But God commendeth his love toward us, in that, while we were yet sinners, Christ died for us" (Romans 5:8).

A God who demonstrates such beautiful love deserves the best we "redeemed beasts" have to offer. And those around us having the beastliness of sin need to be pointed to the beautiful Savior.

God Bless America

Wonderful Time of Year

*I*t is that wonderful time of the year again, we call spring. The sunrise and sunsets seem so beautiful and each day is filled with the love of our Lord and Savor , Jesus Christ.

We have begun preparing the soil in the church garden for the third year and pray that it will again help meet the needs of those around us. Several church friends, neighbors, and relatives have joined together as we turn to God to meet our needs during this financial and spiritual crisis in our country.

It is amazing how we can hold in our hands the little seeds as we plant them one by one, and with proper care and watering, they will grow to enormous plants. From a small seed we get giant size tomatoes, squash, and sweet corn that supply our body with energy in abundance. The better we take care of the garden, the larger the blessings from our Lord and we pray daily for his direction.

This reminds me, when we as sinners decided to take the first step and ask the Lord Jesus Christ to came into our lives. Each day as we prayed and read the Bible, we grew and grew in our faith and wanted to be close to our Lord. We may have dedicated our lives to helping others as a pastor, priest, or missionary. Others may have wanted to serve God in their church as a choir member, deacon, or Sunday School teacher. Then other Christians became homemakers or businessmen and the other opportunities to serve the Lord became enormous.

In addition, we can all share the Good News to friends and those around us, as we help bring this nation back to what the early founders of this great and wonderful country, asked God to bless. We pray you will join other Christians in the church of your choice this coming Sunday Morning.

I might add in our garden we can, plant peas giving us —peace of heart, squash that —squashes our selfishness, lettuce that —lets us really love one another, turnips that has us —turn up and help each other. And I was told do not forget to plant thyme so we will have————thyme for God. thyme for God's Word, and thyme for prayer. —— May God bless this years church garden as we reap in our Christian lives — that what we sow.

God Bless America

Answer to Prayer

The way to reach our Lord is through Christ our Savior, since he is the way, the truth, the life. We should be offering prayers of praise to him and thank him for the Spiritual blessings. Physical blessings , and Material blessings he has given us in the past and the blessings he will supply in the future. He has said he will answer our prayers, however, they may not be always what we think we need at the time.

When we pray to our Lord, we do not need a reservation and he is available any hour of the day, any day, all the days of the year. The line is never busy and we won't be told to call back later.

A young man, 19 years of age, from New Jersey came on a Christian Forum this column reaches out over the internet, and said this is how prayer effected his life.

> *"My 12 year old sister Faith died 2 weeks ago in a car accident. She was a Christian, but I was not. She told me to read the Bible since she was nine. After she died, I was so depressed I was going to kill myself.*
>
> *That is when I tripped over her old Bible. I started to read it to myself, and that is when I found about prayer. That same day I chose to live and keep reading. I became a Christian 2 days before I posted this. Now I go to church and really take the time to pray."*

Several of us on the website sent him messages.

I sent:

> *Sorry to hear about your sister. In the Lord's plan you will always be indebted to your sister for her leading you to the Lord's saving grace. You may as you grow in your faith by reading the Bible and praying find the Lord has big plans for your life.*

He sent back to everyone:

> *Thanks everyone. Now I know Jesus is planning something for me, cause I may not have been saved ever if it wasn't for my sister's passing. Yes, I know now I will see her again. her name is Faith, age 12, 5ft 4 inches, strawberry blonde hair, hazel eyes, and was on a robotics team. You can probably image her.*

I pray this young man will find a place where he can serve the Lord and give his testimony to others.

God Bless America

Easter in Norway

The world celebrated Easter Sunday, the resurrection of our Lord Jesus Christ, in many different ways. When I think of Norway, a land of the Vikings with ice and snow, few people probably know the Norwegians have some of the strangest traditions. Mickey Bambrick, a column writer for the La Conner Weekly News, La Conner Washington, visited the homeland of her ancestors over the Easter holiday, and was really surprised how Norway was so different.

The week before Easter all the schools closed and many people take that week off. Even the stores are only open a few hours each day, and not at all on Thursday or Friday before Easter or the Monday after, which are holidays. About 40% of the population own cabins in the mountains, so that is where they head for the week, and the other 60% join them. While gone they must be sure to have two food items for Easter with them, oranges and a quick lunch bar called "Kwik Lunsj". Also for the past hundred years, they must read a crime novel or two, and the bookstores go crazy promoting all the new Easter released crime novels.

One of the weirdest "traditions" about Easter she found was that most churches were closed on Easter Sunday, because so many people had gone to the mountains. She writes, when I was home in America, we would dress up in our finest, make sure to arrive early to get a good seat, and look forward to worshiping the Lord on Easter Sunday.

We were totally shocked to find the church doors locked and no one around. So we went down the street to another church and found very few people in attendance, with no one dressed in their frilly dresses or finest suits.

After church, as I was preparing a big Easter dinner, I saw a neighbor girl riding her bike, so I hollered out to her "Happy Easter". She looked at me oddly and shouted back "That was yesterday". It was then that I found out another tradition in Norway——Easter dinner and related celebrations happen on Easter Eve.

It is odd, Easter is the celebration of the resurrection of our Lord Jesus Christ, but Norwegians celebrate it while the Lord is still in the tomb. Maybe that's where the crime novels come into play.

God Bless America

Lifes Turning Moment

As Christians, I am sure we can all speak of a time in our life when we felt God was speaking directly to us?

He may have been telling us to change our lives to better serve him; Maybe to speak out to our friends and neighbors about the Lord's wonderful saving Grace, Or to even dedicate our life for full time service, as we follow our Lord in his footsteps, where ever he leads us.

Raised in a Christian home and attending church all my life, when ever the doors were open, and then later with my wife and family, I have always tried to serve the Lord. For the past 50 plus years, I have been living on borrowed time our gracious loving Lord has given me. Because of allowing me to live over the years, he has provided many opportunities to help others and spread the Good News to people everywhere.

With the Lord's help, we have assisted small Christian churches grow by providing bus and van vehicles to start Sunday Morning bus ministries. When I found myself on the radio, I said "Lord where are you taking me?" The Sunday Morning Devotions program of scripture, song and verse went out over three radio stations in the Marysville and Yuba city area of California. Now we have a church garden and provided farm produce to help meet the needs of church members and those around us.

When my wife went home to be with the Lord two years ago, I promised her and our Lord, that I would to the best of my ability help others and continue to follow him where ever he took me. She fully understood and said " I will be watching and know the Lord will open new doors, so you can further serve him.

You may be wondering what happened some fifty years ago that changed my life? God sent me a very strong message that I will never been be able to forget as long as I live. I was in the Air Force in Athens Greece, when my wife came down with polio in 1958. She was sent to an Air Force hospital in Germany and was there several months for treatment. The doctors had me visit once a month for updates and I would fly as a passenger on an AF plane. However, one week there was only a Navy plane going by way of Naples, Italy, refuel, and proceed to Germany.

As the plane arrived in Naples a very large storm came in off the sea, much like Paul described in the Bible. The plane was delayed over six hours before the storm settled down. About a half hour before departing, it was announced for me to go to the terminal office where I was told, "You are bumped off this flight by a person with a higher priority" It has always bothered me and I have many times asked the Lord—Why was I selected to be removed from the plane?. . Our Lord has a roadmap with his plans laid out for us, so I have learned to praise him for the good things and some at the time I think are not so good. Well, the military passenger plane in the fog, crashed into a mountain and all 46 people on board were killed.

I will never be able to serve our Lord enough to thank him for his saving and loving grace to me.

God Bless America

The Family Bible

The family Christian devotions was centered around the family Bible for many generations. During medieval times only the most wealthy families could afford the copied manuscripts. However, after the year 1450 with invention of printing it was possible for families to acquire and to read God's Word. The new acquired family Bible became a place of devotional prayer for family members. A Christian family put their trust and faith in the Lord and the parents were obligated to transmit the faith to their children.

A popular devotion manual published in 1745, recommend family prayer and parental reading of the Scriptures every morning and evening to their children. Since around 1800 all the English versions of the family Bible have included pages dedicated to family history—births, baptisms, marriages, and deaths. Our family has two King James versions of the Bible with the oldest dated 1834 and another published in 1898. They weigh over twelve pounds each and are printed in fine paper with many drawings of Bible stories. It must have helped draw the family together after a day of hard work living on an Iowa farm , to relax and read God's word.

Family Bibles are a unique source for social and religious history, as Christian families raised their children around the Bible. They learned to pray and share reading the Bible when they grew older, as part of the family unit. However, as the radio took over the families attention and then television replaced the radio, we find today Christian families have moved away from spending time together in God's Word.

The words in this hymn titled, "Family Bible" which was published in 1826 and sung in the country churches of the midwest of our nation, I think you will agree has real meaning of Family Bible Devotion time.

"The Family Bible"

How painfully pleasing the fond recollection.

Of youthful connection and youthful joy,

While blessed with parental advice and affection,

Surrounded with mercy and peace from on high,

I still view the chairs of my father and mother,

The seats of their offspring, as ranged on each hand,

And the richest of books, which excels ev'ry other,

THE FAMILY BIBLE THAT STOOD ON THE STAND.

We pray that our nation will turn back to God and we will worship him and bring our families up in the way of the Lord. Trust we will all be in the church of our choice this Sunday.

God Bless America

The Lord is Our Shield

We see in the Bible many references to nature and things around us. Man often would rely on animals for their protection, and would use horses and oxen to provide transportation. We see in Psalm 33-17 to 20, " An horse is a vain thing for safety, neither shall he deliver any by his great strength. Behold the eye of the Lord is upon them that fear him, upon them that hope in his mercy. To deliver their soul from death, and to keep them, alive in famine. Our soul waited for the Lord; He Is Our Help And Our Shield."

Recently we were alerted to a very severe storm headed our way, that would reach us in less than an hour. On our farm, I watched closely as the black dangerous looking clouds rolled toward us with lightning and thunder announcing their arrival. We have seen similar clouds seldom before and after they moved over us, several tornados were sighted and did some damage.

It was interesting to see how our beef cattle, who spend all their days in the open pasture, reacted to a storm of this nature. While the sun was shinning they were contented and leisurely enjoying the plentiful green grass they were consuming. Their calves, all about a month old were laying together and enjoying a snooze in the warm sunshine.

As the storm approached, the cows and the bull kept a close watch on the dark rolling clouds and gradually worked their way toward a row of protecting large trees at the edge of the pasture. When the winds, proceeding the storm, arrived with their howling nature, the bull lead his herd to shelter. Then the mother cows called to the calves to take cover, but I did not see the calves get up and move, even with the heavy winds. Then the first part of the storm arrived with a frosting of pea size hail pelting the ground. The calves must have now realized they were in danger and ran as fast as they could to their mothers for her shield of protection.

How true it is with our lives. We coast along through out our years of living, thinking every thing is sunshine, Then when the clouds of hardship and despair are on the horizon where do we turn for comfort? Do we put our faith and trust in our Lord Jesus Christ to be our Shield against the storm approaching??? Or do we believe we control our own destiny and hope the storm will turn away and give us sunshine for another day?

Our time on this earth is in the hands of our Lord, so we should pray to him and ask for forgiveness and accept his shield of protection from all the storms of life we will be facing. We trust this coming Sunday we will all be praising and worshiping the Lord in the church of our choice.

God Bless America

God Is Dead

That is a startling statement, but last year about this time, we were greeted by highway billboards here in northern California, stating "We Do Not Need God" or God is Dead. " These signs had to have been funded by a well organized group as the cost was probably enormous.

What were they saying in their message to millions of Californians and others that saw the advertisements? Remember we were well into the national depression that was effecting all of our lives, and their message to us came about the same time our President had said "We no longer are a Christian nation to the world".

Where had we gone wrong? Were we in full belief of the statement, which I have never found in the bible, "God Helps Those That Help Themselves"?. Did the signs say we do not need God to get us out of the depression?

Or did the signs say, "God you let us down", when in fact we have let God down and out of our lives for many years. Our great country was founded by God fearing and God praising men but it seems as a nation we have turned away from God after World War 11. We have had generations of prosperity and now think we control our own destiny. We turned to Uncle Sam as the provider of all, and state government took over functions the churches once performed. The education system became a haven for teachers and professors that were against God and the children did not see a home that was Godly, so they were confused as their life moved on.

So today were are we? Are we looking to God for answers and putting our faith in him or are we looking to a bankrupt government system, that is now turning back to the churches for help? Yes, distributing of food to the needy may soon be a function of the churches, with people helping people.

The bible says , Love your neighbor as your brother, and we pray everyone will join together in asking God to lift us out of the hard times we are facing.

God Bless America

God lesses Us With Children

*W*hen the Lord blesses us with a newborn baby it is a wonderful day. We thank him for this child laying in his crib before us and wonder just what will he be. What does his life hold, where will he go, and what will he do? We praise the Lord and in church we dedicate him to the Lord and promise we will raise him in the way of a Christian life.

As a child, he always did well in school and had many friends. I , as his father must have fascinated him with all the fishing tackle, since he wanted to help make, package and deliver the finished product to locations all over northern California. We were close buddies as we traveled life together and he was active in the church attending regularly.

Then when he was a senior in high school, he was stricken with a very rare form of cancer. It was called medullary thyroid cancer and little was know about it. It was always fatal and could not be treated., although doctors of the day, tried everything they could. Our son was in God's hands more than ever and he was fully aware of his fate here on earth, but did not know when the Lord would take him home? I prayed for the Lord's comfort as the Davis Medical Center sent out for help and a doctor was brought in from New York to perform a surgery tried only once before. Over the next 36 months our son had three surgeries performed and he joked to us," Why don't they put in a Zipper?"

Well the doctors told us and our son, they could not guarantee the operations but thought they had eliminated the cancer, and had no where else to turn. He said, "It is in the Lord's hands and I will go ahead and live a compressed life and be ready to go home at any time."

He enrolled in Yuba College, which he graduated two years later with a Business Degree. He married his high school sweetheart, that stayed with him through it all. Mike O'Shea, our family friend, who was one of the top Christian tenor singers of his day, flew back from New York where he was with his group, to sing at the wedding.

Our son was blessed with two sons, but was only able to see and know the oldest. Our son had big plans for a short life on earth and we did the best we could to assist him see the wonderful things the Lord had provided. He went with a group from the YMCA to Oregon and rode the rapids on the Rouge River for a week. He took his first airplane and only airplane ride to Florida to visit his grandparents and they toured all the many sites of interest that area offers.

Then one day, he asks me, "Dad I want to race a stock car." I said, how in the world we going to get that? He answered," At the Marysville Race Track, there is a driver that wants to sell his stock car as he has rolled it twice and the third time is very bad luck, he says." Dad, lets buy it, so we did and I was part of the pit crew. It was still a trying time for my son, as he was heavily bandaged around the middle, but that did not stop him from racing and coming in second on one main event. The other drivers said, How did you do win a final main race coming in second, with a car like yours that no one would race? We prayed often before races and as a pit crew and received help like no other pit crew.

At age 23, my son was told the rare cancer was back and could not be stopped as it spread thorough out his body main organs. He was not bitter and was ready to go home to his heavenly father. Dad he said, I want to thank you and mom for providing a lifetime of living in just five years. I prayed to the Lord, Take me home, and leave my son as he has a lifetime ahead and his family needs him. But the Lord in his wisdom must have decided, I was to take care of my handicapped wife for the rest of our 55 years together?

We do not know how long the Lord has in his plan for us to be here on the earth before he takes us back to our heavenly home. So in the meantime as we praise and worship the Lord, while spreading the Good news to those around us, we can still enjoy all the wonderful blessings the Lord has given us. From College to having a family, and all the exciting activities he enjoyed, our son Gary went home to the Lord a happy Christian.

Trust we will all be attending the church of our choice this week and worship our wonderful Lord.

God Bless America

Easter Sunday April 25, 2011

Easter Sunday is one the most happy days for Christians the world over, as we celebrate the resurrection of our Lord and Savour Jesus Christ. He died for us on the rugged cross and gave his precious blood to save all of us, in our ugly and sinful nature. He was buried and then on the third day arose and now is seated at the right hand of God the father. When he calls us to our heavenly home we will be with him for eternity. The following was submitted by a local pastor, his favorite story, explaining how our Lord loves us no matter how ugly and sinful a life we are now living. All our Lord requires, is we ask for him to come into our lives, repent, and pray, putting our trust in his loving care.

God Bless America

Remembering Father's Day

*L*ast Sunday we honored our fathers, and each of us have fond memories as we helped celebrate Father's Day with the father we love. He was there for us as we went from a small child to the person we are today. Through all our days of happiness and all our days of sadness he understood and stood beside us with encouragement only our father could give.

In my case, my father went home to be with the Lord several years ago. He raised me in a Christian home which I am very thankful, and now I look to my Heavenly Father for guidance and comfort. Our Lord says he will never leave us alone and will always stand beside us though all of life's storms and trials.

Sometimes we go miles to be with our father in his last days before he goes to his Heavenly Home. The nurse at the hospital said "Your Son Is Here" as she escorted a tired, anxious young man, to the bedside of an elderly man. "Your son is here", this time she whispered to the patient. She had to repeat the words several times before the patient's eyes opened.

He was heavily sedated because of the pain of his heart attack and he dimly saw the young man standing outside the oxygen tent. He reached out his hand and the young man tightly wrapped his fingers around it, squeezing a message of encouragement. The nurse brought a chair next to the bedside. All through the night the young man sat holding the old man's hand, and offering gentile words of hope. The dying man said nothing as he held tightly to his son.

As dawn approached, the patient died. The young man placed on the bed the lifeless hand he had been holding, and then he went to notify the nurse. While the nurse did what was necessary, the young man waited. When she finished her task, the nurse began to say words of sympathy to the young man. But he interrupted her. "Who was that man?" He asked. The startled nurse replied, "I thought he was your father".

"No, he was not my father, he answered, I never saw him in my life." "Then why didn't you say something when I took you to him?" asked the nurse. He replied. " I also knew he needed a son, and his son was not here. When I realized he was too sick to tell whether or not I was his son, I knew how much he needed me."

While our Heavenly Father is always with us in our time of need, he also wants us to praise and worship him as we are his child. Trust this Sunday will find all of us worshiping our Lord in the church of our choice.

God Bless America

Praise The Lord

*P*raising our Lord , with prayer, is something we as Christians do each day, as the Lord watches and guides us through this troublesome world. We are reminded that, "Praise ye the Lord " is personal for each of us. No one, even a friend, can praise the Lord for you and you cannot Praise the Lord for me. Sinners can not Praise the Lord as they have no personal relationship with our God. Luke warm Christians will not Praise the Lord as they do not have an up to date relationship with the Lord.

Like God's people in the desert wilderness, they could not keep the mania over to another day. It did not work for them, and it will not work for you and me. We can not live on yesterdays blessings and not Praise the Lord each day as he blesses us. The Lord's blessings may come to us as Spiritual Blessings, Physical Blessings, or Material Blessings and we may not recognize them at the time. When we look back over the years we have been Christians, the Lord's blessings may be the highlights of our life.

We love to Praise the Lord as we see in Psalms 50:23 "Who ever offers Praise, Glorifies me, and to him that order his conversation a right will I show the salvation of God". We pray that each of us are walking close by our gracious and most loving Lord Jesus and are giving him unlimited Praise and thank him for all he has done in our lives.

Trust we will all be worshiping and Praising our Lord, in the church of our choice, this coming Sunday morning.

God Bless America

Church Memories

*O*ver the years, most of us if we moved around the country, have memories of churches we have attended. Having been raised in the corn state of Iowa, where my ancestors arrived in 1855, the Little Brown Church In The Vale has played an important part over several generations of my family.

We don't often think of Iowa as the frontier but the Iowa Territory was indeed a wild place. If you came from the east, the Iowa boat trip would end at McGregor with another three day covered wagon trip to Bradford, Iowa. Abundant fish, fertile soil, roaming deer, fruit trees and free land turned this early Indian settlement into a town. It soon had a good selection of trading stores , including the Dixon Brothers Hardware and stage stop. A doctor moved to town, delighting everyone by using elk to pull his buggy.

By all reports this was a wild frontier town but there soon came a demand for a house of worship. In 1855, a group of citizens organized and chartered the first church which had worship services in homes and stores. The third minister Rev. John Nutting convinced the members that a building was needed. It was always in his mind and heart to build a small house of worship. Land, in a vale outside of town, was donated and timber was cut from adjacent lands. The foundation was laid in 1860 and sills went up. When the Civil War took nearly all the men and most of the income from the church, it remained only a frame. In

1864, some $300 dollars was borrowed and two newly arrived Scotch carpenters, along with soldiers having little connection to the church helped pound nails, and older members were able to finish the church building. My great grandfather was able to help and some of the old tools he used remain in our family .

Church congregations back east sent money and Meneely Bell Factory in Troy, NY sent a bell. The church was painted brown because mineral brown paint was so cheap and the church decided they could use white lead paint later. A visiting carpenter built the church pews at no charge except room and board. The church over the years has struggled with its little congregation and was about to close as did many country churches.

However, in June 1857 a music teacher William Pitts, from Wisconsin passed through Bradford by stagecoach. On visiting , he saw the spot where the town planned to build a church with its oaks and green prairie and flowers. On returning home he wrote a little song he called " Church in the Wildwood". In 1863, Bradford Academy founded by the church, hired Mr. Pitts as a music instructor and his first class sang the song at the dedication of the church building. The song was published by H M Higgins Co from Chicago and ever since has been the The Little Brown Church song. In the late 1800's an evangelistic team made a world wide tour and The Little Brown Church song in New Zealand and Australia became their most popular song. The Weatherwax Brothers introduced the song in the United States and Canada to over 3,000 audiences in the year 1921 and publishers of songbooks and hymnals have included this popular church song for all churches.

People from all over the country go to The Little Brown Church and there have been some 78.000 weddings. My aunt was married there when I was 6 years old and I recall pulling the heavy church bell rope and it lifting me off the floor. Seventy years later on visiting the church I was honored to ring the bell and attend a Sunday morning service. We sang at the closing of the service. The Little Brown Church song.

The last stanza of the song sends a message to all men everywhere to prepare to meet their God.

"There's a church in the valley by the wildwood,

No lovelier spot in the dale,

No place is so dear to my childhood,

As the Little Brown Church In The vale".

"From the church in the valley by the wildwood,

When day fades away into night,

I would fain from this spot of my childhood

Wing my way to the mansions of light."

Three generations of my family attended this small church of 100 members over its 150 years and many are buried in the nearby cemetery.

We trust this Sunday we will all worship our Lord in the church of our choice.

God Bless America

Praise the Lord in Everything.

We find the Bible tells us to give Praise and thank the Lord for everything that comes our way. Thess: 5:18 " In everything give thanks; for this the will of God in Christ Jesus concerning you. " That is easy to do when the answers to prayers are what we had been praying for and wanted to hear. But when our prayers are not quickly answered or put on the side track, or the answer to our prayer was not what we had asked the Lord for, do we still give him the Praise and thank the Lord? Christians have long taught from God's word that all things come from the Lord and we are to Praise and thank him. Only God alone has the roadmap for our life and can see what is best for us, if we only trust him though out our lives.

Over several years I have subscribed to the Mayo Clinic Health Letter (Tools for Healthier Lives) and in the May 2011 issue, there is a number of pages on how to improve your health. The normal things we hear on exercise, eating properly are all mentioned. However, they have now included a section in their own words that is very much like the Bible tells us. The following is quoted.

"Develop a Deep Sense of Gratitude for Life"

"Some people describe gratitude as your moral memory———-a combination of humility, grace, love and acceptance. Each day, identify at least one thing that enriches your life. Living with an "attitude of gratitude" means being thankful for every experience ———Good or

Bad ——-and recognizing those experiences are an opportunity to learn and grow. Let gratitude be your last thought before you fall to sleep at night and your first thought upon awaking in the morning" (end of quote)

Let us all give the Lord praise each day for all the things that come our way and try our best to follow in his footsteps. Trust we will all be praising God in the church of our choice this coming Sunday.

God Bless America

Attending Church

As readers may have noticed, the purpose of this column is to reach out to the people of our area and give them a desire to attend the church of their choice.

As we age it is important that we stay connected with other people. Studies have shown that people who remain socially active live longer, healthier, and happier lives. There are many ways we can become connected with the community and attending church is a prime example. Churches, synagogues and places of worship have groups that organize social events for visitors as well as members. Being a part of the church family and living a Christian life has changed many from a life of despair ——- to a life of hope and promise, trusting our most gracious and loving Lord Jesus Christ.

God expects us to have great concern for our fellow man. We are to learn. to share, pray, and worship together, as we see in: Acts 3:17, " Praising God, and having favor with all the people; And the Lord added to the church daily such as should be saved".

Attending church regularly may lengthen our life. That is what the National Institute on Aging recently reported. Even after taking into such factors as smoking, age and chronic health conditions, older *Americans who attended church meetings each week lived 28 percent longer than those who stayed at home, according to the study.*

Further researchers think that the social support offered by religious institutions may help keep the immune system strong. Indeed, other studies have linked religious attendance to lower blood pressure, fewer cases of stroke, less depression, and better compliance with taking medications.

Many religious institutions offer a variety of special support groups and services (including transportation to church events) to their older visitors and members. Our founding fathers built a nation on "In God We Trust". If we just follow their example, listen to the proven research of doctors, and read God's word for guidance—-we should all benefit throughout our lives and even may enjoy a longer life.

Trust this coming Sunday we will all be attending the church of our choice as we worship God in this great nation.

God Bless America

Three Words We Fear

The thought for today is about three little words that may have sometime in our lives caused us great concern.

The four letter word Lost can give us the feelings of fright, sudden fear, or alarm; when we realize we are truly lost. But when we meet someone to show us the way, Oh, what a wonderful feeling comes over us. When Jesus is there to show us The Way, The Truth, and The Light in our life, we have found a real friend and Savior. We are no longer lost when we put our faith and trust in our Lord and follow in his footsteps.

The word Lonely can make us feel isolated and very unhappy at being all alone. We can at times feel alone even in a crowd of people. We see in the Bible where Hebrews 13: verse 12 says, "Let brotherly love continue. Be not forgetful to entertain strangers, for thereby some have entertained Angels, unawares." If we seek the Lord in our lives we will never be alone and he is only a prayer lengths away.

Now, Rejected is a very harsh word that can affect our well being and health. We can be rejected by friends and even churches we have attended, but our gracious and all mighty Lord and Savior Jesus Christ will never reject his believers. Our Lord tells us in John 15: verses 12 and 13 " This is my commandment, that ye love one another, as I have loved you. Greater love hath no man than this, that a man lay down his life for his friend."

What a wonderful Lord we have if we only look to him for answers. He will lead us from our lost and sinful ways. He will be by our side always, so we are never alone and lonely. We can always call on him through our prayers and he will never reject us or give us a busy signal. The Lord is a friend we can count on all the days of our life, like none we have ever known.

Yes, Jesus Christ is the answer to our needs when ever we feel lost, lonely, or rejected. Trust we all will attend the church of our choice this Sunday and worship and praise our Lord.

God Bless America

Prayer Brings Answers

*T*here have been volumes of writings on prayer and how it brings answers to believers. Over the centuries churches have produced prayer books for members, the Bible has many verses of prayers given to God, and we can give prayers to our Lord on a personal basis. The type of worship and praise we can offer to God in the form of prayer is unlimited. We are his children and and he wants us to pray often and open our day with a prayer. As we see in Psalm 5:3 "My voice shalt thou hear in the morning, O Lord: In the morning I will direct my prayer unto thee , and will look up".

It has been said, Prayer is not a "spare wheel " that we pull out when we are facing trouble. It should be the "steering wheel" that directs us on the right path of life as we follow in the footsteps of our gracious and loving Lord Jesus Christ. When we ask God to solve our problems we have faith in his abilities. However, when God doesn't give us the answer we think we should receive; we should realize God is having faith in our ability to accept a no or maybe later answer. The Lord says he will supply our needs, as he feeds the sparrow, but our wants we are pretty much on our own abilities to acquire.

Sometime we receive answers to our prayers very quickly and other times it may be months or years. Over the past years we have had a large church garden from which we supply produce to area churches and others in need. One year a pastor offered to disc the garden as we began to prepare the soil in the spring. He had lived on a farm and said he was very familiar with a John Deere tractor. We needed the disc attached to the tractor and he proceeded to backup to align the equipment. He missed by a "country mile" on the first attempt and the second try was not much better. After a third attempt, we decided to ask the Lord for guidance and said a short prayer. After the prayer the next alignment attempt was perfect and the tractor using the disc did wonders preparing the soil. Later the pastor said . " maybe we should have prayed first" ? I told him, " maybe God wanted us to know what our prayer would do?"

I might add, when we pray for others, God listens to us and blesses them. We should remember when we are safe and happy, that someone has prayed for us.

Trust this Sunday will find us worshiping our Lord in the church of our choice.

God Bless America

Faith in Our Lord

As Christians who put our faith in our Lord Jesus Christ, we see in the Bible a great verse —Romans 8:28 where God speaks to us. "And we know that all things work together for good to them that love God.

Every day we see and hear those that have great fear of what is happening in their lives and are very negative to what is in their future. If only we put our trust and live by faith in you Lord, we can see things in a very different light. The Biblical position is to believe God by faith—-it is a faith that puts God in charge and allows him to do great things, even miracles. The promise of all things working together for good is not for all men, but those who truly love the Lord, those servants that will do his will—against all odds—-abandon self effort, self pride, and walk in the path our Lord leads us.

Our Lord wants us to put our faith in him, and think positive for what is happening today . The Lord says, I have a plan that may be troubling you today and you do not understand, but it is a positive plan. Only I as God and master of all the universe can see the future. We as Christians, while we now may be in a time of turmoil, understand God will prevail according to his timetable.

Yes, we see the government turning away from God, no prayers in schools, President declaring this is no longer a Christian nation, men posting "God is Not Needed" on highway billboards, no longer a

National Breakfast Day honoring the Lord, and men turning away from churches and or becoming Pastors. Lord you have brought our nation to it's knees with some of the worst times in memory, we are fighting 2 wars, and still you Lord say to think positive. Yes Lord we will follow you all the days of our lives , giving you praise and prayer all the time, as we try to walk close by you.

We know reading your word in the Bible and giving prayers of praise to you Lord, brings wonderful Spiritual Gifts, Physical Gifts and Material Gifts, from you our most gracious and loving Savior. We trust this Sunday we will all be attending the church of our choice and worshiping the Lord.

God Bless America

A Life Change

Several years ago we had on the farm a wooden barn that leaned and was poorly constructed. In it we housed a litter of pigs one cold and windy November. Since the pig litter was only a couple days old we were using a heat lamp. It was blown from its supporting hanger and set the building on fire. The strong wind was blowing the fire parallel to the ground and the barn was a total lost.

Later that year we had built a small red barn made with cement type siding, making it very sturdy and it is not leaning. We now use it as the home for a flock of chickens which thank us daily with numerous eggs.

Every time I pray and praise the Lord for all the spiritual blessings, physical blessings and material blessings he has given, I often think of the two barns and how they were so different.

The old barn was like I was before I put my trust in the Lord and accepted him as my savior. The old barn was left behind and the new barn became my home. However, I have been thinking about how I am today. I have been around a long time, I have withstood a lot of life's storms, I have withstood a lot of bad weather in my life and I am still standing with the help of the Lord.

However, I find myself leaning to one side from time to time, so I ask the Lord to prop me up and protect me from the fires of life. Our gracious and loving Lord Jesus Christ says he will always be there to guide us if we only follow in his footsteps. So we need to pray, " Lord, prop us up on our leaning side so we will stand straight and tall, and Lord we give you all the praise for giving us a building built on the Rock of Salvation."

We trust we will all worship and praise our Lord this Sunday in the church of our choice.

God Bless America

Remembering September 11th

This Sunday, September 11th, is a date in history we will always remember . For me it has two meanings, first it was my wife's birthday, which she would remind me she was here first before the national disaster. Secondly, that day united our country like few other times in history, as we saw how the world's strongest country could be attacked from the outside. We need to pray that our country is also morally strong and will not be attacked from internal enemies attacking our spiritual structure.

We should pray and praise the Lord often that we live in a country that has Freedom of Religion. It has been a freedom guaranteed by our constitution that we can attend the church of our choice and have a personal relationship with our loving and most gracious Lord. The early founders of our country wanted to be sure we looked to God for guidance and even added "In God We Trust" on our coins and dollar bills.

However, many people today feel Freedom of Religion means freedom from religion and do not attend a church or feel a need to serve the Lord. We see men posting messages on highway billboards stating " We No Longer Need God". Prayer has been taken out of our educational institutions and the National Prayer Breakfast was canceled by our president as he declared we are no longer a Christian nation.

I visited the National Sacramento Valley VA Cemetery located near my farm ,where my wife and other relatives are buried. Almost to the tombstone, I noticed a Christian cross marking on them and some had religious verses and comments engraved in the marble stones. If we are not a Christian nation our veterans who protected the freedoms in our country, will disagree. In wartime as they faced all kinds of danger and harm, our servicemen would turn to the Lord for protection and guidance. They even had a song, " Praise the Lord and Pass the Ammunition."

Many of the churches across the nation are having a 24 hour prayer chain on September 11th where they have members praying for our Nation, President, Elected Officials, Pastors/Priests, Church Family, and others. The Bible says in 2 Chronicles Chapter 7 Verse 14: " If my people, which are called by my name, shall humble themselves, and pray, and seek my face, and turn from their wicked ways; then will I hear from heaven, and will forgive their sin, and heal their land."

Trust this Sunday we will all be attending the church of our choice and worship and praise our Loving and Gracious Lord, Jesus Christ.

God Bless America

A Warrior

When we are young and have a life ahead of us, we do not think how war will effect us. Then as we become seniors, we have seen many wars in our lifetimes, and can reflect back on how they have changed our lives. It seems every generation has at least one war with an enemy country that later becomes a good trading partner. We had a world war with Germany and Japan and with their defeat are friendly trade partners today. We had years of cold war with Russia and we now co-operate in space exploration and trade to the benefit of our nations.

We see in the Bible, Matthew 24:6, As Jesus speaks , "And ye shall hear of wars and rumours of wars: see that ye not be troubled: for all these things must come to pass, but the end is not yet". Even today we read of pending wars, but we are told not worry as it is all in God's plan, as He controls the universe. One day war shall be no more...."And he shall judge among the nations, and shall rebuke many people: and they shall beat their swords into plowshares, and their spears into pruning hooks: nation shall not lift up sword against nation, neither shall they learn war any more." Isaiah 2:4

As Christians we are told to be warriors and help spread the Gospel to the those around us and the entire world. We see in Romans 10:15. " And how shall they preach, except they be sent? As it is written, How beautiful are the feet of them that preach the Gospel of peace, and bring glad tidings of good things". Wars will come and go until our gracious and loving Lord and Savior Jesus Christ returns to the earth as the King of Kings . What a glorious day that will be.

When I think of the all most forgotten Korean War of the 1950's, I did not believe I would be called up so went about attending college and then starting a career in accounting. The large business I worked for, placed me in their management training program and I was assigned the accounting department. Most of the coworkers had been in the Army Air Corps during World War II, so heard many interesting combat stories.

Then one day I received an official notice from the Army Recruiter that my number had been called up and was told to go for an Army physical. I passed the physical requirements and was assigned a number and told would be called up in a week or so. On returning home on Friday, I told my folks I was going to join the Air Force, but my mother said it is a waste of your time as they have assigned you a number and you are now Army.

I said a prayer to the Lord and asked for His guidance and then proceeded to the Air Force Recruiting Office. I asked the recruiter if I could enlist and had my education papers with me and he said I looked fit enough and when did I want to leave? I said the sooner the better, and to my surprise he had a group leaving on Monday for California. I thought the farther from Iowa the better so joined the group. My folks saw me off as the bus headed to the Iowa capital, DesMoines, to catch a troop train headed to the far West.

About three weeks into basis training, I was called to the commander's office. He asked just what are you doing in the Air Force, the Army says you are theirs and want you to report to the nearest Army base. I told him I enlisted in the Air Force and the recruiter never asked anything about the Army so I did not offer any information. The Commander and 1st Sgt had a short meeting and returned to ask if I wanted to stay in the Air Force? I said yes, so had me tear off a corner off the message, then the 1st Sgt tore off a corner and then the commander, till it was wadded up and thrown in the trash. The commander said, " Possession is 9 points of the law so, you will stay Air Force. I thanked him and saluted and went back to my join my unit.

The Lord had answered my prayers, and I had a varied career in the Air Force, traveling in all states and many overseas countries. I will never forget this Bible verse: Matthew 21:22, ' And all things, whatsoever ye shall ask in prayer, believing, ye shall receive". I pray our country's leaders will turn to God for answers to our pressing problems just as our founding fathers.

Trust this Sunday will find all of us singing and worshiping our Lord and Savior Jesus Christ in the church of our choice,

God Bless America

Christians Share With Others

When the story about the two brothers ,who owned a well known local grocery story gave everything away, appear in the newspaper we were surprised , but very thankful. Yes, all the contents of their long time business was given back to the community, so I posted it on several Christian worldwide networks. What these Christian brothers did was an act of faith that the Lord would provide for them. They shared with food closets, local churches, even a poor homeless man getting a cart behind his bicycle loaded with foodstuffs, and they freely gave away all the contents . Our small community of Dixon experienced an act of giving that day which will be long remembered.

We see in the Bible Mathew 19: 21 Jesus is speaking to the young man, " If thou will be perfect, go and sell what thou hast, and give to the poor, and thou shall have treasure in heaven, and come and follow me." Richard and Dennis Garcia are human just like you and me, but that day they were God's Angeles to those in need. The brothers provided the Physical and Material needs for many and we pray those being helped will give a Prayer of Thanks to our loving and gracious Lord Jesus Christ.

Here are some of the comments from around the country about this wonderful Christian act of giving we saw and experienced, maybe once in a lifetime.

A man in Lake Worth, FL writes a great story, thanks. A lady in Wennersville, PA comments, I will help within my range, but some are always needy. It is true in some cases you can only do so much, then have to leave the rest to God and just pray for them.

The question presented about Christians being generous brought this from a lady in Asheville, NC, "I have not met a generous Christian". A quick reply came from a lady in Fort Wayne, IN, " Perhaps you did not meet a true Christian?" A lady in Hominy, OK says," Christians are suppose to be generous and some fail because they have greed in their hearts, and some may not even realize it".

A man in Shutesbury, MA wrote:

> *Great story — yes those who realize it is God who has blessed them, Jesus asked the rich young ruler to sell all he had and follow Him, but we know what he did. Seems for some it is too great to give even as it is today with hardships many just look the other way. It is a test of the heart as well as a sign of their faith. God knows and cares for even the least that they might have hope and believe the Lord is our provider and at times uses people who care.*

From Salem, OR a man writes the following an a world wide scale of giving:

> *Diocesan-associated Catholic Charities, Catholic Charities USA is the second largest social service provider in the United States, surpassed only by the federal government. In 2008, Catholic Charities agencies served over 8 million individuals. Catholic Relief Services provides assistance to 130 million people in more than 90 countries and territories in Africa, Asia, Latin America, the Middle East and Eastern Europe. Helping the poor is a priority for the Catholic Church.*

So we see , yes Christians are generous with material goods giving to those less fortunate. We also know man cannot live on bread alone that supplies our body with energy, for we need our spiritual soul part of the body filled with God's blessings also. Reading the Bible, God's word and praying to our Lord daily gives us the spiritual food we need to make our body whole.

Trust we can all be in the church of our choice this Sunday. worshiping and praising our Lord and Savior Jesus Christ.

God Bless America

The Purpose Of God

*O*ver centuries people have wondered, What is the purpose of God and just why he put us here on the earth? We also know that the secret things belong to our Lord Jesus Christ and we must be content to leave them to him. We must not attempt to pry into that which God has not revealed. We see even today where religious curiosity and speculation has killed the zeal and usefulness of many men. Some men have even tried to predict when our Lord will return to the earth and his believers.

It is not for us to speculate about what might happen and why it did not happen. It is our responsibility to bow, to believe, to obey and proclaim what God has revealed to us. We see in the Bible where God tells us in the scriptures his glorious and wise purpose of grace according to which he rules the world. The Book of Isaiah in Chapter 14 verses 24 to 27, God reveals his purpose and should be comfort to all his believers.

In verse 24 we read, "The Lord of hosts hath sworn, saying, Surely as I have thought, so shall it come to pass, as I have purposed, so shall it stand" I do know what ever God's plan is, it will stand forever. His unchangeable, unaltered, and permanent plan he will do at his pleasure for his believers.

In Isaiah we see the purpose of God includes all things. " This is the purpose that is purposed upon the whole earth, and this is the hand that is stretched out upon all nations" (Verse 26) God rules all the nations of the world and all the universe, according to his grace for the salvation of his people. Nothing happens by accident, nothing is determined by man, and nothing is controlled by Satan. God is the ruler of everything, at all times , wherever it happens.

"For the Lord of hosts hath proposed, and who shall disannul it" And his hand is stretched out, and who shall turn it back?" (Verse 27) The Lord our God has a purpose that cannot be resisted and whose power cannot be defeated, as he is God.

Our Lord does what he wills. And this is what he wills — the salvation of his people. We have a God of purpose and we pray that this Sunday will find us all in the church of our choice worshiping and praising of our most gracious Lord Jesus Christ.

God Bless America

Life Is Like A Garden

With fall weather arriving soon there has been a change in the church garden. It only requires some watering and a daily harvest of vegetables, as it continues to produce plenty of squash, tomatoes and cucumbers. The garden may provide for us until the time of a heavy frost in October or even later. By then the winter squash will have been harvested and stored giving us a food supply all through the winter to share with others.

The other day in the early morning, while I was watering the many types of summer squash, I noticed the large leaves on the plants were turning brown and dying. The garden was getting plenty of water so I looked under the leaves and there was new growth sprouting up from the roots. What I thought was a garden dying from drought was really new leaves, new blossoms, and even new young squash, just like a whole new garden was planted.

As I continued to water the plants, a thought came over me. It was just like when we decided to follow the Lord and become a Christian. When we put our trust and faith in our Lord Jesus Christ, we saw the old leaves of our life fade away and as we began to walk with the Lord, a new life sprang up. "Wow, What a Change", Just like the fresh young leaves, the bright yellow blossoms, and the tender new squash, our life changed as we learned to pray and read God's word.

We see in the Bible, Isaiah 58:11 " And the Lord shall guide thee continually, and satisfy thy soul in drought, and make fat thy bones; and thou shall be like a watered garden, and like a spring of water, whose waters fail not". A Christian life is really life changing as we grow in the faith and come to realize the purpose for our lives.

We trust that this Sunday we will all be in the church of our choice worshiping and giving praise to our Lord and Savior Jesus Christ.

God Bless America

God's Phone Number

When we are in an accident that causes major injury or are extremely sick we call 911 to bring a prompt ambulance response to answer our Physical Needs. This is a pretty well developed network of assistance that man has established for the benefit of us all.

When our home is on fire we call 911 to bring the fire department vehicles to our location in a matter of minutes. The firemen pride themselves in a quick response and our insurance rates are based on the response time. This phone number 911, is a man made call network that helps meet our Material Needs.

When we have Spiritual Needs we can make a phone call to our Pastor, Priest, or Rabbi and speak to God's Servant. This call to a man of God most often provides answers we are looking for to relieve our worry and concern in our time of trial.

However, the Bible gives us a phone number directly to God. It is Jeremiah 33:3, yes Jeremiah 333 tells us God will react to our calls. As the Lord says: "Call until me and I will answer thee, can shew thee great and mighty things, which thou knowest not"

Let us meditate and analysis why God is telling the well know Prophet Jeremiah to call him in his time of need? God is not pleased with the conduct of Israel , with the people offering incense on the roofs of their houses to Baal and pouring out drink offerings until other Gods, and God is provoked to anger. He says in Chapter 32:26, "Then came the word of the Lord unto Jeremiah, saying: in the next verses that he going to turn this city into the hands of the Chaldeans and the hand of Nebuchadreszar, King of Babylon.

We see where the Prophet Jeremiah is in prison and it tells us in Chapter 33, the so called book of consolation , that there is hope beyond the national disaster that has befallen the nation of Israel, and destruction of Jerusalem by the Babylonians. Jeremiah has been placed under palace court arrest because his enemies do not like his preaching for the return of Jerusalem and all of Israel to the Jewish people.

While Jeremiah is still in prison for the second time the Lord speaks and says in Jeremiah Chapter 33 Verse 3: " Call unto me, and I will answer thee, and shew thee great and mighty things, which thou knowest not".

The Lord says he will restore Israel, and bring them joy, praise and honor among all the nations of the world, and the other nations shall fear and tremble when they hear of all the goodness and prosperity I have done for my people. Today this small country Israel stands against its neighbors as a beacon of hope and faith in God. Countries that have supported them continued to be blessed by the Lord.

Yes, Jeremiah 33:3 is Gods Phone Number——- We have a direct line to the Lord. It is not just for emergencies but should be an everyday call. The line is always open, we will never get a busy signal, and we don't have to even pay a dime, as it is a local call.

I might close by saying:

I want to thank you Lord for listening to my troubles and sorrow,

Good night Lord Jesus, I love you and will call again tomorrow.

Remember Jeremiah 3:33 - God's Phone Number

God Bless America

GOD'S Wonderful Design

*I*t is fascinating how God has designed the things on the earth for his children I've never given most of this a thought!!!! I do not know the source of this research but would like to share it with all our Christian brothers and sisters.

"God's accuracy may be observed in the hatching of eggs."

For example:

- he eggs of the potato bug hatch in 7 days;

- those of the canary in 14 days;

- those of the barnyard hen in 21 days;

- The eggs of ducks and geese hatch in 28 days;

- those of the mallard in 35 days;

- The eggs of the parrot and the ostrich hatch in 42 days.

(Notice, they are all divisible by seven, the number of days in a week!)

God's wisdom is seen in the making of an elephant... The four legs of this great beast all bend forward in the same direction. No other quadruped is so made. God planned that this animal would have a huge body, too large to live on two legs... For this reason He gave it four fulcrums so that it can rise from the ground easily.

The horse rises from the ground on its two front legs first. A cow rises from the ground with its two hind legs first. How wise the Lord is in all His works of creation!

God's wisdom is revealed in His arrangement of sections and segments, as well as in the number of grains.

- Each watermelon has an even number of stripes on the rind.

- Each orange has an even number of segments.

- Each ear of corn has an even number of rows.

- Each stalk of wheat has an even number of grains.

- The waves of the sea roll in on shore twenty-six to the minute in all kinds of weather. All grains are found in even numbers on the stalks, and the Lord specified thirty fold, sixty fold, and a hundred fold - all even number.

I believe each of us has been designed by the Lord in a beautiful way for His glory, if we will only entrust Him with our life. If we try to regulate your own life, it will only be a mess and a failure. Only the Lord who made our brain and our heart can successfully guide them to a profitable end. Our Lord in His wonderful grace can arrange our life if we only entrusted it to His care. We do not know how long the Lord will have us serve him or when he will call us to our heavenly home.

Hope you enjoy the wonderful things our Lord has provided and we will all be in the Church of our choice worshiping our Lord this Sunday.

God Bless America.

Meditation and Prayer

As we live our lives in this world of turmoil and uncertainty, we often find ourselves spending little time in meditation with our Lord and Savior Jesus Christ. Our days are so crowded with business and our evenings fill with all types of pleasures that the very idea of getting off by ourselves for a time of communication with our Lord is often put off till later. We are so driven by our tasks that we have little time to really live and enjoy the wonders and blessings God has given us.

Our fathers and grand fathers were not so distracted by the world, as they found time and opportunities for thought about things that really count. They did not have TV and they could read serious books and really enjoy reading the Bible. They knew the Bible and fed upon the Word. The family had a Family Bible around which they would gather the family for Meditation and Prayer. We still have the family Bible dating back to 1812 and it weighs over twelve pounds with much of the family history recorded. \

Since Meditation is not mentioned often in our churches of today, we should realize it is not the hasty reading of the Bible. It is the serious — Analyzing, Digesting, and Acting On, the Bible's Holy Truths which makes them sweet and profitable to our soul. It is not he who reads most, but he who mediates most — and really looks into God's Word that makes for a strong Christian.

Meditation is almost like, we become acquainted with heaven before we arrive there and do our best to walk in the footsteps of our Lord, as we raise our families.

We see in the Bible; 1 Timothy 4:15 -16" Meditate upon these things, give thyself wholly to them; that thy profiting may appear to all. Take heed unto thyself, and unto the doctrine; continue in them; for in doing this thou shalt both save thyself, and them that hear thee."

The English King James version of the Bible this year is 400 years old and our country founders some 200 years ago placed their faith in the Lord. We still use the Bible to swear in the leaders of our nation. at all levels of government. In "God We Trust" is found on our coins and dollar bills as this great nation is reminded of Gods gracious love for all of us.

Trust this Sunday will find us praising and worshiping our Lord Jesus Christ in the church of our choice.

God Bless America

Our Lord Answers Prayer

I met a wonderful Christian widow, a young 74 years old, on TipTopWebsite.com/LensLines. where she reads this column. It is one of seven worldwide outlets that the Lord has made available to spread the Good Word to Christians and others with the purpose to motivate readers to attend the church of their choice. We have a most loving and gracious Lord as you will see in the following true story about what God can do if we put our faith in Jesus Christ our Lord and Savour.

We read in the Bible where prayers of faith are important to all Christians that are sick and need healing. — James 6:15, "Confess your faults to one another, and prayer for one another that ye may be healed. The effectual fervent prayer of a righteous man availeth much."

We are on clear across the country from each other but have become good friends. I call her my Fantasy Girl as I have never seen her and may never. Five days ago she played the piano beautifully over the phone and then we prayed together before saying good night.

The next day she called from the hospital in Dallas, Texas and said at the women's church tea she got real dizzy and an ambulance was called, Her blood pressure was 60 over 40 and then extremely high a few minutes later when she got to hospital. Even on the second day the blood pressure was being checked ever 2 hours as it could not be stabilized.

On the second night I talked with her at the hospital and we prayed together that the Lord would put his hand on her and if it was his will, help her. After the prayer, I told her the Lord says, "To be ready to tell the doctors what had just happened, as they will not believe. "

Two hours later the blood pressure was taken and was perfect. 120 over 75. Now, three days later, it is in the same range and has stabilized since the prayer. A cat scan was normal and the lady has recovered her singing voice. She sang Happy Birthday to her granddaughter in a voice she says was like she was in her 60's. She is still a little weak and has had visitors each day from 7AM to 10PM. Her family from the west coast was flying back to see her as friends and family have brought Christian cheer to this kind lady.

Her three sons are in the ministry and all visited today and are praising the Lord for an answer to prayer. I told her it is not what we did but the Lord having a most gracious love for her and he still has plans for her to help spread the Good Word here on earth. A nurse told her that doctors all over the hospital are talking about the results of prayer.

It is wonderful knowing even Christians praying together over the telephone can reach our loving and gracious Lord Jesus Christ when we are in a time of need. We know our Lord still performs miracles of healing if it is the Lord's will. That is why it is important to have Prayer Services at church to pray for our church family and others in need of Physical Blessings, Material Blessings and Spiritual Blessings.

I trust this coming Sunday morning will find all of us singing and praising our Lord in the church of our choice.

God Bless America

Why Go To Church?

We get subject material for Len's Lines from column readers and we really appreciate their response. We try to reach out to people all over the world with the Good Word of our Lord and Savior Jesus Christ. It is especially rewarding to have my brother, a preacher in Iowa, send this story on Why We Should Attend Church.

He says a Church goer wrote a letter to the editor of a newspaper and complained that it made no sense to go to church every Sunday. "I've gone for 30 years now," he wrote, "and in that time I have heard something like 3,000 sermons.. But for the life of me, I can't remember a single one of them... So, I think I'm wasting my time and the pastors are wasting theirs by giving sermons at all."

This started a real controversy in the "Letters to the Editor" column, much to the delight of the editor. It went on for weeks until someone wrote this clincher:

> "I've been married for 30 years now.. In that time my wife has cooked some 32,000 meals. But, for the life of me, I cannot recall the entire menu for a single one of those meals. But I do know this.. They all nourished me and gave me the strength I needed to do my work. If my wife had not given me these meals, I would be physically dead today. Likewise, if I had not gone to church for nourishment, I would be spiritually dead today!"

When you are DOWN to nothing... God is UP to something!

FAITH sees the invisible, believes the incredible and receives the impossible! Thank God for our physical and our spiritual nourishment!

This is one of his favorite sayings which I think everyone should read. We all face challenges every day, but our Lord stands besides us, and the Lord says he will never leave us. This we read in the Bible, Hebrews 13:5 Let your conversation be without covetousness, and be content with such things as ye have, for he hath said, I will never leave thee, nor forsake thee.

"When Satan is knocking at your door, simply say, "Jesus, could you get that for me?"

We trust this coming Sunday, we will be in the church of our choice, singing and worshiping our Lord Jesus Christ.

God Bless America

God Even Blesses Us With Eggs

Readers of this column have asked me what church I attend and I answer, I am a Christian first and then attend a church with a name given it by man. Since I am a country boy, my choice of a church is one where I can serve the Lord and feel I am walking in the footsteps of Lord.

Our country church is located in a very small town that was once the railroad connection junction for surrounding larger cities . The church now sits only yards from the mainline transcontinental railroad line from back east to the San Francisco bay area. The church reminds me of "The Little Brown Church in the Vail" in Nashua, Iowa where my great grandfather help build and attended in the 1850's. However, this church has survived by members staying loyal to God's word, singing the old fashion gospel songs and reading the King James version of the bible. The preacher is a God fearing man and a pastor in every sense. We go into the church with its seven pews on each side with setting of maybe a hundred to sing praises and worship the Lord and we leave inspired to go out in the world and serve. A train going by while we are singing, adds volume to our praises and if one passes while the pastor is preaching it gives a live moving background to his sermon.

The pastor says this is the year we are going to reach out to those around us and spread the TRUTH. He gave us car bumper stickers that read, "GOT TRUTH" and our church name. Our small church attendance is increasing in both the morning and evening services as we see new faces and greet them each week.

Recently the pastor started a Christian College Scholarship Fund so we could assist our fine young people go to a Christian College and learn to serve the Lord on the mission field or as a pastor. We give the evening offering on the 5th Sunday of each month towards the fund. We have also asked the Lord to show us additional ways we can add to the fund. My sister in law and I have been giving brown eggs to church members from our farm as we as a church family like to help each other. With the new fund, we prayed how we could help and the Lord has given us one blessing after another.

My Christian companion wanted some more chickens so we went to the feed store and she selected 10 baby chicks, I want this one, this one and so on. We expected some would die and some be roosters as in the past. However, the Lord blessed us with all the chicks becoming hens, and not loosing any chicks. Now they are brown hens and just beginning to lay. It is almost winter, but we are getting dozens of eggs every week to give to our church members. All we now ask is that they but in the pastor's scholarship fund a donation, that they would normally spend for eggs at the market.

We are blessed giving the eggs and knowing they will add to the fund and the ones getting the eggs are happy and also blessed knowing they are helping add funds to the scholarships.. It may not be in large amounts but it is giving from the heart and I am sure our young people will see the funds the Lord has provided them to help attend school came from caring church members.

Our church may not be large in size but we are trying be a shinning beacon of TRUTH to the lost world both here and with our outreach, around the world. Hope you will attend the church of your choice as I do each Sunday and we will sing and worship our most gracious Lord Jesus Christ.

God Bless America

Christians Help Others

*T*his column welcomes subject material and appreciates articles that reach out to our readers around the world. This story subject is from the Pastor's Pen, by Pastor Gerald Harder and reminds us how the Lord works through us, the Christian children of God.

The pastor says:

> *"The world is a better place because of the Person of Jesus Christ. We see in the Bible in Acts 10:38 "How God anointed Jesus of Nazareth with the Holy Ghost and with power, who went about doing good..."*

Those that have known and lived the principles of Christ have done incredible good. Consider the many universities in our country formed for the express purpose of preparing young people to serve as pastors, missionaries, and teachers. These great schools were founded by Christian people for Christian purposes. Think of the many hospitals, orphanages, care homes, and the like with Christian names.

Social ills, such as slavery ended largely by the efforts of committed Christian people who championed the claims of Jesus.

The pastor comments, " An Atheist guest in a homeless shelter once commented, " I do not like the way religion is shoved down our throats"——- even though no one was forced to attend the rescue mission services. The Christian worker replied, "Why don't you go to the atheist's rescue mission?? The guest replied, " Where is it?" There is not any ——Atheists do not care about rescuing anybody but themselves."

We thank God for the wonderful Christian people of all different church groups in the world that do good in the name of our gracious Lord and Savior Jesus Christ. Recently we have been contacted by Christian readers of this column from, Canada, Argentina, Fiji Islands and Australia and look forward to hearing from readers in other parts of the world. The Christian bond we have for each other makes us a Christian first and then we unite with church groups we are comfortable with ——-having a name man has attached to the congregation.

We trust this Sunday will find us all attending the church of our choice , where we can sing and worship our most gracious and loving Lord Jesus Christ.

God Bless America

Remembering Thanksgiving Day – A Day Of Giving

Once a year we have set aside a day, for a national holiday of giving thanks to our Lord, for all the wonderful things he has provided us in the previous year. We gather together with relatives and friends for a meal to remember with all the turkey and trimmings. A prayer is offered up to our Lord and Savior, Jesus Christ as he gives us everything for our everyday needs.

As we have concern for our fellow man and give to him our abundance, as we are able, a good feeling comes over us . Love our neighbor as our brother has been the policy of all Christians and our wonderful nation is there helping others in this world in a loving manner time and time again.

We read in the Bible, II Corinthians 9 verses 7 and 8; "So let each one give as he proposes in his heart, not grudgingly or of necessity, for God loves a cheerful giver. And God is able to make all grace abound toward you, that you, always having all sufficiency in all things, may have an abundance for every good work."

My widow sister in law, who helps me on the farm and is my Christian companion, said her aged almost 90 years young mother would like a mincemeat pie for Thanksgiving. Being of English ancestry, she would once before going home with the Lord, like to again taste a mincemeat pie. We visited or called every large grocery store, bakery and talked to friends and was given the same answer. Mincemeat pie is not a good selling item in the area so we decided a couple years ago to eliminate it from available special order pies. However, in Dixon we were told a new specialty cafe, called the "Firehouse Bistro" might help us. We went there but the sign on the door said. "Closed For Remodeling". The owner saw us and opened the door and said they will be open for business later in the week. I said you are our last resort and we hope you might be able to bake us two mincemeat pies, but see you are all torn up remodeling. He asked how soon we needed them and they would sure like to help us. So today, two days later. we became the first specialty home baked pie customers with two beautiful English Mincemeat Pies. The owner even told us the history about the English Mincemeat Pie he had researched. There is no meat in them today, but years ago in England, wild game, Moose or Deer was a part of the pie. For Thanksgiving Day, we delivered the pies out of town today, the aged mother of my relative had tears in her eyes.

Our small town of Dixon has some wonderful merchants and we pray for the success of this creative comfort food cafe and specialty bakery called the "Firehouse Bistro". Our Thanksgiving Day will long be remembered by the caring cafe owners who went out of their way to make us a mincemeat pie, a real Christian act of giving.

We pray you all had a wonderful Thanksgiving Day and we will all be in the church of our choice praising and worshiping our Lord Jesus Christ.

God Bless America

Prayer is Powerful

Each day as Christians, when we offer up prayers to our loving and gracious Lord and Savior Jesus Christ, we are using the most power tool the Lord has given us. We may not get the answer right then we are asking the Lord to provide but he says in the Bible, Matthew 21 verse 22. " And whatever things you ask in prayer, believing, you will receive."

Over the past couple years, I have been visiting a senior medical home for persons recovering from various operations, and take my two Cavalier King Charles Spaniels to greet them. After a few times of visiting patients, I ask if they attend church and would like to pray? One aged lady, who said she was told that before she could go back to her home might be up to another month, said I would like to pray but do not know how. She said after attending church all her life, she had others in the church pray for her when she wanted to ask the Lord for something. I told her it was just like you and I talking, so we prayed that the Lord would lay his hand on her, if it was his will, and bless her with his healing power. The next week, when I went to visit the senior home, the kind Christian lady was gone. The nurses said, she even surprised the doctors with her quick recovery and her son picked her up to go home yesterday.

We get answers to this column about the Power of Prayer from readers and this touching letter was received from a Christian lady in Florida.

Hi Lens Lines,

Here is a true story which occurred approximately 20 years ago about 1991.

I was teaching school at Springhead Elementary School in Plant City , FL at the time. Each day on my way home to our "farm" of ten acres in the country, I took highway 39 and drove north out of the city to the country. Highway 39 divides a grave yard with graves on the right and left side of the highway.

It was about 4:30 pm and the sky was over cast. As I drove though the grave yard portion of the highway I could see a man standing with his back to the highway and leaning over a tomb stone. I could not make out who was but was impressed to pray immediately for him. The remaining 5 miles of my trip I prayed for this stranger that God would send someone to talk to him to minister to him.

The next afternoon my son, John came to our house. He told us that his wife had left him and taken their son. He then told me that he had gone to the grave yard the day before contemplating suicide. He said that as he was leaning over a tomb stone a man dressed in black and carrying a Bible called out to him and visited with him for a long time and read Scriptures with him. And then as quickly as he had come he disappeared.

When I asked the time he said about 4:30.

I have no idea if is was an angel that God used to answer this prayer or if it was a human that God moved to minister to my son, it really makes no difference.

> *The point is that God answers prayer and we as His children should always pray for strangers along the highway. It may even be one of our loved ones.*
>
> *Blessings,*
>
> *Donia*

We as Christians see prayer answered in our lives daily, if we only pray in faith and trust our Lord Jesus Christ to answer. Trust this Sunday we will all be singing and worshiping our Lord in the church of our choice.

God Bless America

Act Of God

When we think of all the things that happened in our lives, we often recall what the world believes are an Act of God. Yes, earthquakes, floods, tornados, and droughts are not under our control, so they must be an Act of God. We have no control, and even our home insurance which covers fire and robbery, has extra charges for earthquake, floods, and other Acts Of God.

We pray that God will be merciful on us as we have recorded numbers of earthquakes, floods and natural disasters around the world in this past year. Some men in high places, tell us we can have control over the world by actions we take , such as the warming of the earth. God has a plan for his universe and his people, and only God knows the answers to this worlds difficulties. If we look to our Lord and Savior Jesus Christ, we can rest assured that what ever comes our way is in his plan for our lives.

Now, let me tell you this story and see what you think? When I retired from the Air Force in 1973, living in Marysville, California, Texaco offered me a service station to operate and it was doing fine. Then we had this so called gas shortage with individual rationing of odd and even number license plates that effect all of us. As a service station owner we were also rationed and it was based on the previous years gasoline sales volume. The previous owner was a mechanic so cared little about gasoline in his business but this had a dire effect on my business.

Each day, I would sell the meager amount of gasoline and then post an Out of Gas Sign. When the local newspaper made a survey of how the service stations were dealing with the shortages, then found me resting with my feet on the desk and sort of down in the dumps. They ran a story on my predicament as a veteran with a family with four children facing this personal disaster. TV Channel 12, in nearby Chico, California ran the story a few days later but Texaco was not able to do anything.

One day, I called the Texaco dispatcher and asked if anything had changed, His answer was, " I wish you would stop calling me and I am telling you to get more gas will have to be an Act Of God"———- I said I believe you are right.

I was no longer discouraged and would again go to the Lord in prayer. In the Bible our Lord says in John 14 verses-13/14, " *And whatever you ask in My name, that I will do, that the Father may be glorified in the Son. If you ask anything in my name , I will do it"* As I prayed I remembered reading the morning paper where a new Dept of Energy, had been added to the President's cabinet, in Washington DC. So I called and a man answered saying, "I have only a chair and a telephone as desks have not yet been delivered. What may I help you with"?

After listening to my story, I told this unknown kind man, that I have been praying and he was my only possibility of getting any relief from the rationing quota. He answered, You will hearing from me soon and I thanked him for listening to my story.

I sat back down and about two or three hours later the phone rang, and to my surprise it was my Texaco dispatcher in Sacramento, California saying a full load of fuel has just left headed to you. By the way, who do you know in Washington D.C. that works for the Dept of Energy, as not only is this fuel load coming to you, they also took you off the rationing quota giving you all the gasoline you can sell? I said it was an Act Of God, as he answers our prayers if we ask Him and it is His will. A couple weeks later Texaco asked if I would operate a second service station in Marysville, which I accepted and thanked the Lord for His gracious love of his believers.

Trust this Sunday will find us all in the church of our choice praising and worshiping our Lord and Savior Jesus Christ.

God Bless America

Christmas Is All Around Us

*I*t is that time of year, Christmas, and it gives us a great feeling. We see Christmas lights on many of our homes and we see Christmas wreaths on doors everywhere. Beautiful Christmas trees brightly shining out of windows reflect the love of our families and the Christmas spirit. As we see our local businesses decorated and the Christmas lighting the city has installed, it reminds us of all the wonderful things people do at Christmastime.

We help with Toys For Tots, warm coats for our children and Christmas meals for our seniors, as we share with others in the Christmas tradition of love thy neighbor as a brother. We see the thousands of hero's graves decorated with Christmas wreaths at our local Sacramento Valley VA Cemetery, as we remember those that have given so much to protect our freedoms.

Christmas brings out the best in us as we think back on all the wonderful times we have enjoyed with family, friends, and the interesting strangers we meet at Christmas gatherings. Hot chocolate and cookies help keep us warm as we join others singing Christmas carols to the homebound, but the Christmas spirit and a warm coat keeps us going.

We see our local churches celebrating Christmas with special services and helping those in their time of need. Yes, Christmastime is when we reflect on the true meaning of Christmas, as we celebrate the birth of our Lord and Savior, Jesus Christ.

The English word Christmas means Christ's Mass, the festival of our Savior and Lord Jesus Christ which we celebrate on December 25th each year. The first Christmas celebration was recorded in 336AD and started by the Romans as the known world under their control became Christians.

When someone greats us with Happy Holidays, we are quick to respond with Merry Christmas.

We hope the wonderful Christmas spirit remains with us all through the coming year as we look forward to the challenges and the blessings we will all be facing in our wonderful Dixon community. Trust we will all be in the church of our choice worshiping and praising our Lord this Sunday.

God Bless America

The Meaning Of Christmas

We as Christians would like to believe the world is celebrating Christmas, the birth of our Lord and Savior, Jesus Christ. In some respects that is true, they may recognize the holiday Christmas, but it maybe in just a holiday spirit.

Here in this great land of ours, blessed so many times by the Lord, even our President says this is no longer a Christian nation based on how many regularly attend church. We see our public schools no longer allowed to celebrate with Christmas Programs, many restrictions on public display of Christmas themes, and the government at all levels trying to make Christmas politically correct.

Why is it the world so despises the reason we celebrate Christmas? Why does our culture try to replace the word Christmas with, Happy Holidays or even XMAS? You ask me, and I believe it is because we are so self centered, so sure we can do everything on our own, and we no longer look to the Lord for our needs. However, we now are finding we and the government can no longer take care of our everyday needs. Our Loving and Most Gracious Lord is there to pick us up in our time of need, if we only put our faith in him. He asks, that we as his servants, recognize his birthday, Christmas with its true meaning.

We see this year good news in some areas at Christmas time. The largest retailer chain has announced this year according to spokeswoman, Linda Blakely, that WalMart will be greeting customers with "Merry

Christmas" early and often. Also Sears, will be placing up Merry Christmas Banners and changing their advertising to reflect a Christmas theme. Other national chains are rethinking their past policies on removing Christmas from their stores.

So this year let us not be silent about why we celebrate Christmas. While it is great to share gifts with each other and have a happy feast celebration, let us remember the inspiration for gifts comes from our Lord Jesus Christ. Jesus came from his glory to earth to be like one of us, a tiny, helpless, baby. He gave himself to die on the cruel cross so that we might live, as without our Lord in our lives we have no hope of salvation.

Let us remember if someone greets us with "Happy Holidays" we will return a warm greeting and quickly respond with "Merry Christmas".

This Sunday, Christmas Day, let us all turn out in record numbers and fill the church of our choice as be sing and worship our loving and gracious Lord, Jesus Christ, on his birthday.

God Bless America

Spreading the Good News

Well, with God's Grace we made it to the New year. What a wonderful feeling, with all the peace, comfort and strength our loving Lord and Savior Jesus Christ has provided us to face the world each day.

You may be wondering who this old man is that writes this religious column each week? Does he walk the walk or just talk the talk? I wonder the same as I try to walk in the footsteps of our Lord and Savior. However, we as Christians all fail in our daily lives but our Lord Jesus Christ picks us up and carries us through the rough times. He says in Hebrews: Chapter 13, Verse 5 "I will never leave you nor forsake you." and Verse 6, "So we may boldly say, "The Lord is my helper; I will not fear, What can man do to me." What a wonderful assurance of salvation, if we only put our trust in the Lord Jesus Christ and live by faith.

Our Lord has given each of us a talent by which we can serve him and spread the Good News to the Lost, Lonely and Rejected in this world. It may be as a servant of the God serving in full time service as a Preacher, Priest or a Missionary, or maybe serving him as a Sunday School teacher or in the Choir. There are so many ways to serve as we pray for the Lord's direction and turn our life over to him.

Some wonder why I do not have my picture as part of the column heading to identify me as the writer? I want to give the Lord all the glory and credit, as he tells me what to write each week. and I am just trying to be his humble servant. Yes, the writer could be any Christian man, who has given his life to the Lord and wants him to be first in his life. You may see him anywhere, at the Post office, in the local store, attending a church service, Mass or prayer meeting and this could be the writer?

As we look at our lives, do we reflect the way our Lord wants us to live each day? Are we an example to those around us, helping and serving those in need of encouragement? Are we only Sunday Christians and blend into the sinful world the rest of the week so as not to be noticed?

We can help by tilling the soil, planting the seed, and our loving and most gracious Lord and Savior Jesus Christ will be there to bring in the harvest . Let us this New Year reach out to those around us and try, as best as we can, to offer prayer, material help, and spiritual guidance using our God given abilities he has provided his believers.

Pray this Sunday we will all be in the church of our choice worshiping and praising our Lord and Savior, Jesus Christ.

God Bless America

The Traveling Evangelist

Recently we were honored by having a traveling Evangelist and his wife visit our country church. He preached as our pastor was on vacation that week. What a blessing, this young couple with their wonderful singing and piano playing, really energized the congregation. It brought back memories of the Evangelistic Tent meetings we had when I was a kid in Iowa, part of the Bible Belt of America.

In those days the city churches would put aside their doctrine differences and really worship the Lord. A large Circus Tent was obtained from somewhere and erected in a enormous empty parking lot. The floor was covered with wood shavings, the sides of the tent was raised up to provide a cooling cross wind (hopefully), a place was arranged for the choir and a small band to be seated , and advertising was posted everywhere.

A few days later the Revival Meetings began and the whole town turned out. Some people made into the tent, others stayed in their parked cars, and still others listened from nearby home porches. It was an event everyone looked forward to and brotherly love was flowing like a river. Our large church for several weeks after the Revival Meeting was filled every Sunday morning and if we did not get there early we had to sit in an overflow area of folding chairs. The Lord seemed to bless us everyday and we were in the great depression.

In those days there were not the many government programs as we have today. We looked to our loving and gracious Lord Jesus Christ for our support, as in the Bible it says he will provide our needs, as he feeds the sparrow.

We find the word Evangelist is primarily found in the New Testament and is a verb " To announce the Good News". We find in the Gospels, Jesus is presented as the first preacher of the Good News of the Kingdom of God, Mark 1 14-15 and Luke 20-1 In our more modern times the word Evangelist has developed a more specialized meaning of a traveling preacher or revivalist. Like others in the Bible who have followed in our Lords footsteps, today we can all tell the Gift of Salvation to those around us , even if we can not sing and preach like a true Evangelist.

Trust this Sunday will find us all in the church of our choice, singing and praising our Lord Jesus Christ.

God Bless America

Is ASAP Our Way Of Life

Our life as a Christian is in constant change as we face the challenges of everyday. We like to see our Prayers to our Lord and Savior answered ASAP, and we are often impatient to see the results.

Sometimes we may be talking to a friend and mention that ASAP we plan to do that this or that. Then again we may be faced with an impending danger and call for assistance to come to our aid ASAP. When it was an emergency team coming to our aid, they arrived ASAP which is their model of responding.

We often speak of a plan to our spouse, " Let us do this ASAP and that may make us both happy as we look to the future. " Yes, the ASAP set of mind often brings results to our lives and we pray it is all in God's plan, as only He has the roadmap of our lives.

Now, when we think we are the one in charge of everything, we can find ourselves at times greatly disappointed with our failures and limitations. Sometimes when everything is going our way, we may think WOW , We did it on our own and we forget God is in charge of everything that comes our way. Whether it is what we desire or his plan for us, we should praise and thank HIM every day.In everything, we can rest assured and find peace and comfort in our lives if we try to follow in our Lord's footsteps, by praying often and reading God's word the Bible.

Now let us put ASAP in a less demanding definition instead of need to be concerned type of crisis. ASAP should be our first response to all of life's decisions and challenges in today's hurried world. What a comforting feeling comes over us as a Christian knowing we have a constant friend that will never leave us. Even if we stumble and fall our Lord is there to pick us up and even at other times he carries us through life's troublesome waters until we can get our feet on dry ground again.

Lord, we thank you for your Mercy and will come to you each morning in Prayer and during the day ASAP. Our first thought should be " ALWAYS SAY A PRAYER" in all our daily activities, whether facing danger or planning for the future. We know prayer to you, our Lord and Savior Jesus Christ, brings Physical Blessings , Material Blessings and Spiritual Blessings that are showered on us believers. *We read in Jeremiah 33 verse 3, " Call to me and I will answer you, and show you great and mighty things, which you do not know."*

Let us put our faith and trust in our Lord Jesus Christ and join in the church of our choice this coming Sunday as we worship and praise Him.

God Bless America

Are We Included In God's Plans

Over centuries people have wondered, What is the purpose of God and just why he put us here on the earth? We also know that the secret things belong to our Lord Jesus Christ and we must be content to leave them to him. We must not attempt to pry into that which God has not revealed. We see even today where religious curiosity and speculation has killed the zeal and usefulness of many men. Some men have even tried to predict when our Lord will return to the earth and his believers.

It is not for us to speculate about what might happen and why it did not happen. It is our responsibility to bow, to believe, to obey and proclaim what God has revealed to us. We see in the Bible where God tells us in the scriptures his glorious and wise purpose of grace according to which he rules the world. The Book of Isaiah in Chapter 14 verses 24 to 27, God reveals his purpose and should be comfort to all his believers.

In verse 24 we read, "The Lord of hosts hath sworn, saying, Surely as I have thought, so shall it come to pass, as I have purposed, so shall it stand" I do know what ever God's plan is, it will stand forever. His unchangeable, unaltered, and permanent plan he will do at his pleasure for his believers.

In Isaiah we see the purpose of God includes all things. " This is the purpose that is purposed upon the whole earth, and this is the hand that is stretched out upon all nations" (Verse 26) God rules all the nations of the world and all the universe, according to his grace for the salvation of his people. Nothing happens by accident, nothing is determined by man, and nothing is controlled by Satan. God is the ruler of everything, at all times , wherever it happens.

"For the Lord of hosts hath proposed, and who shall disannul it" And his hand is stretched out, and who shall turn it back?" (Verse 27) The Lord our God has a purpose that cannot be resisted and whose power cannot be defeated, as he is God.

Our Lord does what he wills. And this is what he wills — the salvation of his people. We have a God of purpose and we pray that this Sunday will find us all in the church of our choice worshiping and praising of our most gracious Lord Jesus Christ. God Bless America

God Bless America

Do Christians Laugh

*A*while ago I posted this subject on a Christian website and the answers were very extensive. They ranged from straight laced Christians that thought no laughter was permitted in the church to other Christians that felt the church should be full of laughter and joy.

We see the first reference in the Bible to laughing in Genesis 21:6, And Sara said, " God has made me to laugh, so that all who hear will laugh with me." Verse 5 tells us, " Now Abraham was one hundred years old when his son Isaac was born to him." His wife Sara was eighty years of age, so we can understand her concern, but she put her faith in the Lord.

In Job 8:21 we see Job speaking that God will do this for his believers. " Till He fill thy mouth with laughter and thy lips with rejoicing."

King David speaks of his people that are serving the Lord in Psalm 126:2, " Then was our mouth filled with laughter and our tongue with singing. Then they said among the heathen, "The Lord has done great things for them."

From these Bible verses I believe we as Christians can rejoice with laughing when the Lord is first in our lives and we listen to his word as he speaks to us. It has been determined by many medical studies that laughter is great for our health as it reduces stress and provides us a more enjoyable way of living.

However, we see in the Bible book of Ecclesiastes were King Solomon tells of all his greatness and how he has gained more wisdom than all that were before him in Jerusalem. He further says ' My heart has understood great wisdom and knowledge." As a preacher he says in Ecc 2, verse 2, " I said of laughter—It is mad, and of mirth (pleasure) , What doeth it?".

He adds in Chapter 7 verse 3, " Sorrow is better than laughter, for a sad face the heart is made better".

From this some have determined that the preaching of Solomon in the Old Testament is meant to mean we should not laugh and rejoice in the Lord's House but remain attentive with straight faces as we worship and sing praises to our living Lord and Savior Jesus Christ.

Now, The New Testament of the Bible after Lord Jesus gave his life on the rugged cross, shedding his blood to wash away our sins, we should be rejoicing and enjoy the wonderful life the Lord has provided us.

As Christians we read where Jeremiah the Prophet, speaks of the Lord's message to him after the people turn back to the Lord. It applies today in our country as we seem to have lost our compass and must again seek the Lord for direction. The Lord speaks to Jeremiah in Chapter 30 Verse19, "And out of them shall proceed thanksgiving and the voice of them that make merry, and I will multiply them and they shall not be few, I will also glorify them, and they shall not be small."

Trust this Sunday we will all be in the Church of our choice worshiping and singing praises to our Lord Jesus Christ.

God Bless America

Church Music and Instruments

*R*ecently my church had a guest piano player and her husband brought a real Rams Horn from Israel. It is known as the SHOFAR by the Jew and blown on Rosh Hashana and other special occasions. He blew it very softly in the church and it sounded different than anything I ever heard as a band player. Later after church he gave us the full sound treatment outside and was it loud, and I mean loud. I can see why the Bible says the earth shook when a King was installed if dozens of Rams Horns were used.

When we look at the music in early churches it is very interesting. Even today churches are being torn over what type of music to use. The larger churches are even having two services with separate music for each service. Smaller congregations are blending both types of music in their services.

We go to church to get instruction and fellowship, however, we also go to church to worship the Lord. The traditional worship has been through singing praises to the Lord. If we feel left out in the singing, as many today in the churches with the nontraditional songs, some believers become followers of TV Church Services and stay home.

The development of music and its use in early Christianity is found in the New Testament, but covers only a very short time span. In general it seems that music of the early Christians, was like that of the synagogue, entirely vocal. (Mark 14.26, Acts 16.25) and consisted mainly of Psalms (1 Cor. 14.26)

In the Old Testament and the last Psalm 150 -3 we find " Praise Him with the sound of the trumpet, praise him with the lute and harp. Verse 4, Praise Him with the timbrel and dance, praise Him with stringed instruments and flutes. Verse 5, Praise Him with loud cymbals, praise him with clashing cymbals. Verse 6 Let everything that has breath Praise the Lord."

I believe we praise the Lord with all of the music instruments mentioned in Psalm 150, but not all in the church. We find not all the instruments listed of that day. It lists the— Strings (Lyre and harp with 10 strings)— Wind Instruments, (Ram's Horn and flute) but not the metal trumpet — Percussion Instruments (Tambourine and cymbals) but not the sistrum drums. The non listed had other purposes as seen in coronation of Kings (Samuel 19.35) (1 Kings 1.40, "The noise of pipes and trumpets was so great the earth quaked" David brought the Ark to Jerusalem in a religious procession of dancing, shots of joy, and sound of the Ram's Horn. (2 Samuel 16-19) The blowing of the silver trumpets both summoned the congregation to the temple and indicated the time of offering-sacrifice. To the accompaniment of stringed instruments (Ps 98.5) the priestly choir sang hymns of Praise, Petition, and Thanksgiving.

The Psalms are known as the Hymn Book Of the Second Temple. By the 4th century , music had became an important part of worship and continues to be one of the ways believers worship the Lord in today's services.

We trust this Sunday will find us all worshiping in the Church of our choice and singing praises to our Lord.

God Bless America.

What Is The Value Of A Lie?

*T*hink we can all recall a time when we said it was only "A little white lie." about something? Oh! we may have even thought, it didn't matter. it was just a small lie. How small is small and did it effect someone? How did we feel after telling a lie and did it make us feel better? I have often wondered why we call it a White Lie as a lie is a lie. Maybe it even grew and became a different colored lie?

The Bible tells us as Christians in Colossians, Chapter 3 Verse 9-10, " Do not lie to one another, since you have put off the old man with his deeds, and have put on the new man who is renewed in knowledge according to the image of Him who created him".

Many years ago, I was faced with a decision that I can remember very well and it could have changed my life. It even makes me uncomfortable thinking about it some fifty years later but I praise the Lord he carried me through the rough waters of temptation and put my feet on dry ground.

While living in Greece, I was involved in an automobile accident when driving through Athens. As I waited for a signal to change the accident happened right before my eyes and it involved me. A large dump truck was crossing the intersection and a small car went through the red stop light opposite where I was waiting and collided with truck. The truck driver swerved towards me, as he attempted to keep from getting hit, and struck my car on the drivers front corner. The collision drove my car backwards and I was thrown about. My elbow went through the drivers side glass window but I was not too badly injured, so did not go to the hospital. All the broken parts of the car grill were recovered and my 1956 Chev was reassembled Greek style. They did wonders fixing and pounding out the damaged fender until it was like new.

The accident was scheduled to go to traffic court a few weeks later. To my surprise I received a phone call from the attorney representing the driver of the small car . He asked what I saw and I told him in detail that the driver of the truck accidentally hit my car as he tried to avoid having a major accident with the small car. He was glad that my car had been repaired and wanted me to do something for him.

The attorney asked that I tell the judge a totally incorrect version of the accident, that his client was not responsible, and the truck was operated in an unsafe manner. After explaining over and over just what he wanted me to say to the judge in traffic court, he added , if you do as I tell you , we will do this. — I will give you $3,000 US dollars and you can say it was for pain and suffering. I told him "I would think about it".

When the Court day came, I prayed again and the Lord said Christians do not lie, even if you might gain, and although it did not effect you, others would suffer. I told the truth on the witness stand and the truck driver and his wife and kids I could see were all smiles. Later the attorney called me and said you agreed to our story, but I reminded him , that I would consider it and as a Christian I could not knowingly lie. He said he would make life difficult for me and my family and my Greek auto insurance was canceled. The American Embassy told me if the newspapers carried an unfavorable story, that I and my family would be out of Greece in 24 hours.

The newspaper article told how an American serviceman stood up to the temptations of the powers to be and they gave a good account of the court actions. My Greek neighbors came over and thanked me as did the truck driver and his family. The Embassy covered my auto insurance until I could find another source. and we as a family stayed in Greece another two years. When the truth was known, the little car was driven by The Wife Of The Mayor Of Athens, Greece.

I could never have been comfortable living with that lie, Maybe it could have been classified as a "Little White Lie" at the time but I am happy today that the Lord spoke to me in firm words, that many years ago.

Trust this Sunday will find us all worshiping our Gracious and Loving Lord Jesus Christ, in the church of our choice,

God Bless America

I Found The Answer

*Y*ou maybe wondering what I found the answer to? Was it how to make a fortune in the stock market or in real estate deals, running the farm or growing a productive church garden and sharing with everyone? Yes, all of these things can be an answer to some of our goals in life, however, I have found that a life to be successful and rewarding must have a higher goal than worldly things. We will not be satisfied and have that inter peace until we have accepted our Gracious and Loving Lord Jesus Christ as our Savior and He becomes the King Of our life. A life of being a servant to our Lord and serving Him with our God given talents is the answer to what we have been searching for all our lives.

I would like to tell you about my life long Christian gospel singing friend, Michael O'Shea who had a beautiful "Irish Tenor" voice that touched the hearts of thousands of people through his ministry of singing and music. I met him in the early 80's when a young college group, the Light Ministries visited our large church in Marysville. California and he was their lead older adult singer. He appeared in person on a live Christian Radio program " Sunday Morning Devotions" that I had on three radio stations and was a blessing with his music and testimony. I was honored to have Michael stay at our home for a week and learn how the Lord had changed his life.

Michael was born in New York City. in an Irish part of the city, and grew up in a poor family. During high school he played baseball and with singing developed his tenor voice. After graduating he was accepted on the NYC police department and all the while he rarely attended church with his family. He was going to be a self made man and rise out of the situation he was raised. While playing on the police baseball team he was recruited by a scout for the Los Angeles Angels. a national major league team on the west coast. While playing he still developed his singing voice and became known as the Tenor Baseball Player while singing in local gigs. While there was found by Hollywood scouts and asked to be in several movies, with Dean Martin and Jerry Lewis, and another with Lloyd Bridges, Michael said at that time I thought he had found the answer he was looking for and entered the Hollywood doorway to his life. He married a well known movie actress and lived the life with a big Hollywood mansion, that was part of a TV series on how the Movie Stars live. He was living his life the way he wanted to and he could now show the world how to succeed all on your own. But we see in the Bible how pride is treated , Proverbs 16. verses 18 and 19, " Pride goes before destruction. And a haughty spirit before a fall. Better to be of a humble spirit with the lowly, Than to divide the spoil with the proud."

In a matter of time he found himself losing his beautiful home in Hollywood, expensive living style and even his family split with his wife and daughter leaving him. Sure he could still sing with his Irish Tenor voice and he traveled the country from coast to coast singing at worldly groups and nightclubs. He wondered often why had he lost it all but the Lord never was a part of his life. As age added years on his life he wondered what he had to live for. Then one day he visited his daughter and the grandchildren he had never seen in Redding, California. He saw a Christian home, it was so much different and even found himself attending church after all those many years. While there his daughter told him he was just a shell of a man, living a terrible life and she had been praying for sometime that he would see the answer to life was with Jesus. That next Sunday in church, Michael O'Shea, accepted the Lord as his Savior and that night was baptized as he made a public confession of faith in our Lord and Savior Jesus Christ to the whole world. It was an answer to prayer and Michael left his sin world behind and gave his burdens of the past to the Lord to carry and he started a whole new life serving the Lord.

Often times we hear Christian music singers and we wonder if the message is real. Each song he sang had a tremendous message right from the heart with real feeling and love for the lost as he reached out to them He had now found real peace and loved to quote to everyone John 14-6. " I am the way, the truth and the life, no man comes unto the Father but by Me. " Michael says he had now found the answer to life and it has a purpose. I told him, before he went home to be with the Lord, how he had been the best of friends all those years, how I appreciated him flying back from New York City while on tour to sing at my son's wedding and I wished I could have done more to help in his ministry. He became a Christian man late in his life but the devil lost the battle and we also can all live a life for the Lord, if we put our Hope, Trust, and Faith in the Lord and repent of our sins. He is there to reach out His loving arms to us what ever our condition and carry us to the higher ground. Thank you Michael O'Shea for being a part of my life and we strengthen each other as Christian brothers, and we found the answer to life.

Trust we will all be in the church of our choice this Sunday worshipping our gracious and loving Lord Jesus Christ.

God Bless America

When Will God Sing?

As we live our daily lives each of us spends time praying and reading the Bible, God's word for guidance. We also gather with others as we attend the church we select to sing and worship our Lord and Savior Jesus Christ. We reach out to others around us and spread the Good Word to those that should be saved, so they also can know the wonderful life and Salvation that is available to those that put their faith in the Lord.

All this is good that we do as a person serving the Lord, however, What about our nation—Do we still honor God? Our country forefathers established a nation made up of colonies each worshiping the Lord and was established under those guidelines. We see "In God We Trust" on many public buildings and on our money, bills and coins. The Bible is used to pledge our trust in God, as our office holders at all levels of government lay their hand on God's Word.

We read in the Bible, in Mathew 25 Verse 31 to 34, " When the Son of Man, comes in his Glory, and all the holy angels with him, then he will sit on the Throne of His Glory. " All the nations will be gather before Him, and he will separate them one from another, as a shepherd divides the sheep from the goats. " And He will set the sheep on His right hand, and the goats on his left. "Then the King will say to those on His right hand, "Come, you blessed of My Father, inherit the kingdom prepared for you from the foundation of the world."

In our lifetime, we have seen the nations that have fallen away from serving God, no longer the leading nations of the world. They have suffered greatly in times of war, disaster and a demised standing among other nations. Our country has been blessed time and time again, however, there now seems to be movement away from serving or even needing God's protection and guidance. Are we headed down the slippery slope other nations have taken?

I pray not, For God can bring severe punishment on nations as we see in many places in the Bible. One such reference is in the Book of Zephaniah were God was very unhappy and destroyed the nation of Israel. When they repented and prayed for His forgiveness, we see our Loving and Gracious Lord was willing to accept them back under his protecting wings. We even note He Sang.

Zephaniah 3-17 tells us, "The Lord Thy God in the midst of thee is mighty, He will save, He will rejoice over thee with joy, He will rest in His love, HE WILL JOY OVER THEE WITH SINGING.

Yes, if our nation turns back to God for his guidance, we will see a God that sings with us as we worship and sing in the church of our choice this coming Sunday.

God Bless America

Showers of Blessings

*B*lessings are showered on us as we see in the Bible, Ezekiel 34-26, "I will cause showers to come down in their season, there shall be showers of blessings".

We may not even recognize a Blessing as they come in the form of Physical Blessings, Material Blessings, and Spiritual Blessings. Some of us may have even said , I never get a Blessing and have stopped asking the Lord. We may have blinders on our eyes and cannot see the small Blessings, as we look to the Lord for that enormous earth shaking Blessing we have always wanted.

The Lord may have said I will supply your needs, However, your wants are up to you to obtain. As we look back over our Christian lives we see many Blessings that the Lord has provided us and we praise him for his comfort and guidance as we try to follow closely by his side.

Our loving and gracious Lord Jesus Christ, tells us in Matthew, Chapter 5 verses 3 to 10: "

> Blessed are the poor in spirit, For theirs is the Kingdom Of Heaven.
>
> Blessed are those who mourn, For they shall be comforted,
>
> Blessed are the meek, For they shall inherit the

earth,

Blessed are those who hunger and thirst for righteousness, For they shall be filled.

Blessed are the merciful, For they shall obtain mercy.

Blessed are the pure in heart, For they shall see God.

Blessed are the peacemakers, For they shall be called sons of God.

and Blessed are those who are persecuted for righteousness sake, For theirs is the kingdom of heaven".

Now that is many Blessings of all types, and sometimes the Lord even takes back a small Blessing and gives us a much larger one in its place.

Recently on my small farm, I had a calf born and it was a Blessing. It was rather small and not able to nurse so was bottle feed, as we sometimes have had to do in the past. It was doing fairly well but when the rainstorm came through it became weak and died. I prayed what to do with the cow as could only keep so many on the pasture, The Lord answered to sell the cow and another large cow that did not have a calf, but I thought that will take time. That day I went to a neighborhood market and mentioned my problem to the owner who said his brother was looking for a cow for beef. They would be over to see the cows in a day or two, he said, so I went home, prayed and took a nap.

I was awaken by a knock on the door, and there were the brothers to look at the cows. They bought both cows and paid for them and we shook hands to seal the agreement. Yes, the Lord may Bless us with small Blessings and take them back and give us a much larger Blessing.

Pray we will all be in the church of our choice this Sunday singing and worshiping our Lord and Savior Jesus Christ.

God Bless America

Pray For A Safe Journey

*I*n this busy world, Do we look to our Lord in prayer for a safe journey through the path of life? Are we following in the footsteps of our Lord down the roadway he takes us or do we sometimes stray into the wilderness. If we continue to put our faith and look to Him whenever we stray, Our Loving and Gracious Lord is there to receive us back under his protecting arms. Our daily prayer and reading of God's Word the Bible, gives us a wonderful personal relationship with the Lord of our Salvation.

We see in Matthew 7- where we must ask the Lord for his guidance and protection, Verses 7-8, " Ask and it will be given to you, seek, and you will find, knock, and it will be opened to you. " For everyone who asks receives, and he who seeks finds, and to him who knocks it will be opened to you".

When ever or where ever we plan a journey through life our travel plans should not be complete until we pray for the Lord's guidance. He may want us to delay or even cancel our plans as He knows best and we cannot see the future. Being in the service many years ago, my travel plans were set by the Air Force, but I still prayed to our loving Lord for his protection on a trip that was full of adventure and might hold unknown danger.

As the plane winged over the Mediterranean Sea, high above the beautiful blue sea, the trip was enjoyable. They had sent me as a member of an inspection team to Adana AFB, Turkey. for the next month. The base runway is one of the longest so the pilot flew the aircraft, a C-54 four engine prop just above the runway for some distance. Then he cut the engines and the plane dropped hard on the surface and blew two tires on one side, causing swerving and a very rough landing. I thanked the Lord for a safe flight and was put up in a cabin type tent, as the base was still undergoing construction. The area is only some 20 miles from the birthplace of Paul the Apostle , in Tarsus , and I was able to cross the Roman Bridge in use today that Paul used to begin his travels.

The inspection went as planned and when finished I had no travel established to return to Greece, so the transportation officer set up a trip across Turkey. First, was 2 days by a coal burning steam train, going through 27 tunnels with the smoke coming in the train windows. On arriving at Ankara, the capital of Turkey, the train was late, so was rushed to join the plane at the end of the runway before it left. The THY (Turkish Airlines), was an old DC-3 and we had a rough storm ahead which caused the passengers a lot of grief as we passed through. I prayed knowing the Lord was in control, and went to sleep only to be awaken by the hostess fearing I was in trouble. The aircraft landed safely in Istanbul, a seaport city, where I was to catch a BEA (British European Airways) plane back to Athens.

This plane was the latest in that day, with turboprop engines, and I looked forward to another peaceful trip over the beautiful shinning sea. The next day as we rolled down the runway for takeoff an engine failed and the pilot was able to bring the plane to a stop just short of end of the runway and the awaiting water of the sea. We waited 3 days for another engine to arrive from London, so was able to visit the area. The flight home to Greece was uneventful and I thanked the Lord for a safe journey and his protection over that eventful month of my life. We never know what lies a head as we travel through life but it helps to have the Lord as a travel companion.

May we all join in praising and worshiping our Lord Jesus Christ in the church of our choice this Sunday.

God Bless America

Trust

Where do we put our trust as we go through life with all it's turmoil and dark and gloomy times? Are we one that says, "I do not trust anyone but myself?" "I can gather many riches and be self sufficient in my time of need?" Then again, we may put our trust in a friend who we think will always stay by us. Or maybe we are saying, " I put all my trust in the government as they will take care of me?"

Did we ever notice that even our forefathers realized they were not able to make decisions with all their knowledge available without turning to a Higher Authority? On our coins, money, and official buildings we see the words of our nations founders as they looked for guidance. Our country has been successful in many ways because we have a Partner we can trust. Yes, IN GOD WE TRUST, is everywhere we look in our nation and God has been good to us in His blessing of nations.

We see in the Bible where our Lord Jesus is telling his disciples and others that were listening, Mark 10 verses 24-25: "Children how hard is it for those who trust in riches to enter the kingdom of God! "It is easier for a camel to go through the eye of a needle than for a rich man to enter the kingdom of God".

So we can see that riches, friends, and government are not the answer we are seeking. They may help us in the immediate short time but over the long haul, only our loving Lord and Savior Jesus Christ is the answer. The Son Of God, who shed his blood on the cross for our salvation , if we put our trust and faith in Him, He will carry us over our times of need.

One of these days we will all lay down our physical body to rest and leave it. Our spiritual body lives on in eternity forever, and pray we will all be in the Hands of our Gracious and All Mighty Lord and Savior and be rejoicing by His side.

Trust this Sunday will find us all in the church of our choice, worshiping and praising our trusted Friend and Savior Jesus Christ.

God Bless America

Easter

aster Sunday, the most important religious day in the Christian community, is a day of giving. We celebrate this day by attending our church, see the display of Easter Lilies, give Happy Easter greetings to everyone, and share an Easter meal with family.

Our Lord , Jesus Christ gave us the greatest Gift of all time. He was the Christian Passover Lamb, as He laid down His life for our Salvation. Our loving and most gracious Lord gave us a spiritual eternal life by His love for us, we see in the bible, I Corinthians 5-7 "For even Christ, our Passover, is sacrificed for us"

In the Old Testament we see in Isaiah: 53-7 " He was oppressed and He was afflicted. Yet, He opened not His Mouth; He was led as a lamb to the slaughter". This was told many centuries before God sent his Son in the form of a Man to provide for us the way as Gentiles to become God's children. If we put our trust and faith in our Lord Jesus Christ, who offered Himself for us, we begin a spiritual life and find an eternal presence with Him in Heaven.

In the Gospel according to John, we see were he writes where Jesus dies on the cross according to the Gospel's chronology. It was a time when the Passover lambs were being slaughtered in preparation for the feast. John 19 Verse 31.we read : "Therefore, because it was Preparation Day, that the bodies should not remain on the cross on the Sabbath. the Jews asked Pilate that their legs might be broken and that they might be taken away". —-but when they came to Jesus and saw He was dead already they break not his legs—- but pierced his side".

With the permission of Pilate, we see where Joseph of Arimathea, (a disciple of Jesus) and Nicodemus in verse 42, " So there they laid Jesus, because of the Jew's Preparation Day, for the tomb was nearby". Then we see in John 20- verse-1 " Now on first day of the week, Mary Magdalene went to the tomb early, while it was still dark, and saw that the stone had been taken away from the tomb" In verse 17, Jesus said to her. "Touch me not, for I am not yet ascended to My Father, but go to my brethren and say to them, "I am ascending to My Father and your Father, and to My God and your God."

Easter is therefore the Christian Passover, and has been observed by the early Christians on Sunday. This is owing to the Lord's resurrection on the first day of the week, which is strongly suggested in the New Testament evidence. It is a wonderful day to celebrate the greatest gift that ever has been given to all mankind by our loving Lord and Savior Jesus Christ.

Trust this Easter Sunday we will all be in the church of our choice, singing and worshiping our wonderful Lord and Savior.

God Bless America

Heavy Burden

When we are facing a burden of some type and it has become a heavy load on our person, how do we handle it? Where do we turn for relief from our pressing problems?

It could be a physical medical problem we are experiencing? Yes, doctors and medicines may have the answer, however, do we pray for the Lord's helping hand to guide them and give us a fast recovery?

There are several references in the Bible as we see in Psalms 55- verse 22: "Cast your burden on the Lord as He shall sustain you".

The burden maybe a material need that seems so large, as we face it? It could be we are searching for work or even facing a home foreclosure that gives us enormous concern. We as Christians, do we look to our loving and most gracious Lord Jesus Christ in prayer for his guidance?

Then maybe we are facing a spiritual crisis and seek counseling from our pastor to direct us? Our prayers to the Lord on a personal basis for all our needs will lighten the burdens we are carrying. Our Lord says in the Bible, Matthew 11 verses 28 to 30: " Come to Me, all you who labor and are heavy laden, I will give you rest. Take My yoke upon you and learn from Me, I am gentile and lowly in heart, and you will find rest for your souls, For My yoke is easy and MY burden is light".

I recall this story, as if it was yesterday , while living in Greece years ago. A driver and I took a large military type heavy duty truck from Athens Airport, where we were assigned, to the American Embassy located across the city. We had a load of supplies to deliver and it was a normal duty day. On the way we noticed a large city bus had stopped and all the riders where on the outside. They were trying to lift the heavy bus and I told the driver Jim, let us stop and see if we can help in any way,

Under the bus was a small boy and his bicycle and they could not be removed. We quickly raised the bus with our 10 ton heavy duty jack that we carried in the truck. The little boy was rushed to the hospital by a waiting taxicab as no ambulance was on hand. The bus riders and crowd of on lookers, began a chant—-Bravo Americanos, Bravo Americanos and the bus driver thank us. We went on our way having lifted the burden and had a good feeling.

Let us look to our Loving and Most Gracious Lord, Jesus Christ whenever we are facing a burden. Prayer brings Physical Blessings, Material Blessings and Spiritual Blessings if we put our trust in Him and walk in His footsteps.

This Sunday, Let us attend the church of our choice and worship and praise the Lord as he continues to lift our burdens.

God Bless America

Plans

As we go through life, we have often laid out our plans and pray to the Lord for His guidance. We may go ahead and make all the arrangements and believe everything is going well as scheduled. We may not have had a positive answer from our loving and gracious Lord Jesus Christ, however, we feel we will get an answer from our Lord before the date of the planned activity.

If we proceed with our plans on our own, we see in the Bible where even our Lord speaks of Nations and peoples plans. Psalms 33-4 "The Lord brings the council of the nations to nothing, He makes the plans of people to no effect".

I think all of us can remember in our lives times when the Lord changed our plans, maybe cancelled a trip, or told us no in His own way to our well laid plans. Then the Lord often gives us a reason why He took the actions that we thought at the time were not in our best interests.

Recently, we called the farm butcher to place on his schedule a day and time he could arrange to come on the farm. We wanted to butcher a bull while it was still tame as we have a young bull calf for next year as a replacement. He gave us a time and date. We arranged for the same day to have a grandson disk the garden area. The weatherman said rain was predicated later in the day but we would have all the activity accomplished before noon. For a couple days we prayed to the Lord for a successful day that we had scheduled.

On the morning of the planned activities, by 9AM there was a steady downpour of rain that soaked the ground and put all planned activities to a halt. The butcher and his crew had arrived and said it will be another week, as rain is predicted for area all this week, so we will call you a new date. I called my grandson it would be another week or more before it will be dry again, as we cancelled the disking of the garden.

I felt discouraged that all the planning had to be cancelled. But the Lord has plans for us that we do not see or can even imagine will effect us and those around us. Even the farm animals are in His plan, as the Lord is ruler of the universe. we see in the Bible: Psalms 36-6 " Your rightness is like the great mountains; Your judgments are a great deep; O Lord, You preserve man and beast".

Later in day, I went out to feed the chickens and noticed the cattle all in a huddle and calves, some a week old, in the middle. The bull was guarding the cattle and had his head to the ground looking as big as possible. Around the cattle were circling coyotes as I watched and yelled at them, but I was ignored. After several minutes the coyotes left leaving one, but he finally decided to leave as he faced the bull. The guardian was there when he was needed as our Lord had cancelled the days planned activities.

We did not know or understand the way of our Lord as He does His will. . Our plans and prayers are in His hands as we place our trust, hope and faith in our Savior and Lord Jesus Christ.

Trust this Sunday will find us all singing and worshiping our Lord Jesus Christ in the church of our choice.

God Bless America

Miracles

As Christians in our prayers do we ask the Lord to do miracles for us? Are we putting God to a test or are we asking Him to put His healing hands on us, if it is His will?

Scripture in the Bible in several places tells us where Satin wants to put God to a test of His power. We see in Matthew 4 Verses 3-4: Now when the tempter came to Him, he said " If You are the son of God, command that these stones become bread." But He answered and said," It is written, man shall not live by bread alone, but by every word that proceeds from the mouth of God."

Almighty God does not need us, as His servants, to put to test his plan for our lives. We should give Him all our trust and faith as we pray to our loving and most gracious Lord Jesus Christ. When we pray and in prayer meetings call on the Lord to hear our needs we should be sure it is Biblical or we are in danger of putting God to a test. If it is His will we may receive blessings that are Physical, Material or Spiritual. The Lord my even give us a miracle that we did not expect, if it is His will.

Many years ago, our son who was 19 was in the hospital in Sacramento, for adrenal cancer . They brought in a doctor from New York, as it was a rare type of cancer. After the operation our son went into a coma for three days and we stayed by his side most of time. On the 3rd night, the doctors said we want you to go home. His vitals are failing and we do not expect him to live through the night and we will call you. We had earlier called our pastor and a prayer chain was started by church members calling other church members for prayer. My wife and I were ready to accept the Lord's will for our son Gary and went to bed and had a sound sleep. Around 3 AM the phone rang and my wife said do you want me to answer it? I answered the phone and began laughing as the nurse said, Your son is sitting up telling jokes to the nurses giving us an uplifting spirit. I said, Praise The Lord as it was His will to lay His healing hands on our son. We did not ask God for a miracle but He gave us one.

Trust this Sunday morning we will all be in the church of our choice, singing and worshiping our All Mighty Lord and Savior Jesus Christ.

God Bless America

Teach Us To Pray

We as God's children are blessed with the opportunity to go to the Lord in prayer. Even though we are not Kings, Queens, or a person of power we can go directly into the throne room of God with our prayers. He is never to busy to hear our prayers, does not limit the subjects, or give us a time period that we can talk to our loving and most gracious Lord Jesus Christ.

Some Christians have said. I do not know how to pray. We see in the Bible, where the disciples of the Lord after listening to Him pray asked for guidance and instruction for prayers. Luke Chapter 11 and verses 1 to 4, " And it came to pass, as He was praying in a certain place,, when He ceased, one of His disciples said to Him, "Lord, teach us to pray, as John also taught his disciples."

So He said to them " When you pray, say:

Our Father which art in heaven, Hallowed be thy name,

Thy kingdom come, Thy will be done, As in earth, so in heaven,

Give us day by day our daily bread.

And forgive us our sins, for we also forgive everyone that is indebted to us.

And lead us not into temptation, but deliver us from evil."

We can see our Lord asked His Father in prayer for a variety of needs that cover a wide range of subjects. Our Lord knows our needs and the problems we face in this sinful world from day to day. Wow, the least confident child of God, can at anytime, any place, or in any situation, come into the presence of the Lord and have assurance, boldness, and confidence that their heavenly Father will hear their prayers.

Let us not forget this promise of the Lord: 1 John chapter 5, verses 14 and 15, " And this is the confidence we have in Him, that, if we ask anything according to His will, He heareth us. And if we know that He hears us, whatsoever we ask, we know that we have the petitions that we desire of Him."

Pray this Sunday we will all be in the church of our choice singing and worshiping our most precious Lord and Savior Jesus Christ.

God Bless America

Whom Do You Serve

As we go through the many aspects of our life the question often comes up, "Whom do we serve?' Some people may even say, I serve no one, I am my own boss. Others like to think they make their own decisions and are accountable to no one.

Let us take a look at this question and sort of take a view of it in depth and what the Bible has to tells us regarding servants. We read in Matthew 25 verse 21, Jesus speaks" His lord said to him. " Well done, good and faithful servant, you were faithful over a few things, I will make you ruler over many things. Enter into the joy of your lord."

If we are in business, we soon learn we are a servant to the customers. The military has a chain of command, making us subject to orders from above, as we do our service for our country. Even the President is a servant of the people in our form of government. We are all in some way a servant to others around us and as we serve them, to the best of our abilities, we find ourselves having a wonderful feeling of satisfaction.

We see in the old Testament, where prophet Moses was a servant all his life. Deuteronomy 34 verse 5, " So Moses the servant of the Lord died there in the land of Moab, according to the word of the Lord". And in Joshua 1, verse 1, "After the death of Moses the servant of the Lord, it came to pass that the Lord spoke to Joshua.

The Bible is filled with wonderful passages of Godly men and women being the servant of our loving and gracious Lord and Savior Jesus Christ. We can also be a spiritual servant of our Lord if we put Him first in our lives. He says to knock and I will open the door, ask and you will receive, as He blesses us with Physical, Material, and Spiritual Blessings. As His servant we know, our Lord , ruler of the universe, is the most wonderful Master. He supplies us with all our needs and we are just everyday Christian servants trying to follow in His footsteps, as we go through the trials and tribulations we face each day. We thank you Almighty Lord for listening to your humble servants, answering our prayers, and giving us guidance.

We pray each of us will on Sunday be singing and worshiping our Lord Jesus Christ in the church of our choice.

God Bless America

Spring Season Is Wonderful

*I*t is that most wonderful time of the year, that we call spring. The trees with all their blossoms are so beautiful and each day is filled with the love of our Lord and Savior Jesus Christ.

Now for the fourth year on the farm, we have begun planting the church garden and pray that it will again meet the needs of those around us. With the help of church members, neighbors, and relatives; we join together as we turn to God to supply our needs in this time of material and spiritual crisis in our country.

As we plant potted tomatoes and corn, summer and winter squash, we are happy to see eight wild geese wing low over us and land in the pasture with the cows. Then the calves came to the garden fence to see what we are doing and we hand feed them alfalfa cubes. Nature is all around us, as God shows us the marvelous things He has created.

It is amazing, as we hold in our hands these little seeds and plant them one by one, that they can grow to enormous plants with our loving care. The more attention we give to watering and weeding, the more we are blessed with a productive garden. But our Lord tells us we must wait patiently as He controls the growing cycle and the rains., as we also await the return of our Lord Jesus Christ.

The Bible says in James Chapter 5, verse 7, " Therefore be patient brethren, until the coming of the Lord, See how the farmer waits for the precious fruit of the earth, waiting patiently for it till it receives the early and later rains".

This reminds me of the time we decided to take that first step and ask the Lord Jesus Christ to come into our lives as our Savior. Each day as we began to understand the Bible and pray, we grew and grew in our faith and were walking closer to our Loving Lord Jesus Christ. As we attended church, we found loving care was extended to us by other Christians as they helped us grow closer to the Lord. Our new found faith began to bubble over and we then shared the Good News with others.

It is just like the garden that supplies our physical body with food, as a truly saved Christian we are supplied spiritual blessings. May I add in our garden we can plant Peas,—giving us a piece of heart, Squash that will squash our selfishness, Lettuce that really lets us love one another, and Turnips that helps us turn up and help each other. May God bless this years church garden and remember we reap in our Christian lives— exactly what we sow.

Pray each of us will be in the church of our choice on Sunday singing and worshiping our Lord and Savior Jesus Christ.

God Bless America

Let Us Look To The Lord For Answers

We read in the papers where our country is turning away from worshiping our Lord and Savior Jesus Christ. Even on our highway billboards around the country, we have posted signs saying – God Is No Longer Needed. We have taken prayer out of our schools; some of our leaders believe they can pass laws to solves all our social issues, and even our President has stated this is no longer a Christian nation and is for Gay Marriages.

Where are we headed as we see world religious figures of all Christian denominations saying prayers for our country. We see in the Bible, II Chronicles Chapter 7 Verse 14, " If my people which are called by my name, shall humble themselves, and pray, and seek my face, and turn from their wicked ways; than I will hear from heaven, and will forgive their sins, and will heal their land."

It may seem like we are all doing our own thing and not looking to our Lord Jesus Christ, for His wisdom and guidance. Things to us as Christians may look very bleak and gloomy, but we should not fear for the Lord, the Master of the Universe, is in charge and has a plan. He may not reveal it to us, then again he sometimes gives us a small view of things to come.

We as Christians should keep on believing and keep on trusting for He is holding us in His hands and will never leave us. We are seeing some states, in the Bible Belt of our country and other states, holding to the Biblical beliefs of our founding fathers. Our founders realized they needed God's guidance to establish this nation, and the Lord has blessed us over the years.

We see from statistics religious families have more children than secular humanists have children , if any. The first gay marriage state , Vermont has the lowest fertility rate in our nation and this means millions of progressive men and women will leave no generational legacy.

From this we may see a trend that is clear; God has a plan We are headed for a far more conservative and religious future in this nation, in which traditional values will make a comeback. We praise the Lord for His gracious love and understanding of our concerns.

We see in 2 Corinthians Chapter 6 Verse 17,18, " Wherefore, come out from among them and be separate, saith the the Lord. and touch not what is unclean thing , and I will receive you" and I will be Father unto you and you shall be My sons and daughters. Saith the Lord Almighty."

Let us all join in the church of our choice and sing and worships our Loving and Gracious Lord and Savior Jesus Christ this coming Sunday.

God Bless America

Spreading The Gospel

Some of the early church missionaries are in our history books, however, we do not think of them in that manner. We see in the Bible where Jesus tells his followers in the book of Mark, Chapter 16, verse 15 , " And He said unto them, " Go ye into all the world and preach the gospel to every creature."

By the 4th century, Christianity had become the prominent religion in the Roman Empire. In time Europeans were Christians and their countries began to seek routes to the East for spices without going over land through the Muslim countries. They also wanted to expand to the newfound areas of the world as European countries were rapidly becoming over populated. The Christian way of life was superior to the customs of the natives of lands and evangelism was the Biblical goal. so they sent explorers out around the world. It was a dynamic Christian outlook and spreading the Good Word lasted longer than the years of exploring for new routes to the East.

Many of the explorers I have researched, had a Bible in one hand, with a desire to convert the heathen , and a desire for riches and fame in the other. The churches of that time always stressed the importance of reaching the lost, so the explorers had a double aim in their journey and asked God for His protection , as they set out on an unknown and possible dangerous adventure.

We see the celebrated and great explorer Christopher Columbus was God fearing and asked for His help. According to those that were with him, as his journal has been lost, he read the Bible to the crew. When the rough seas about two days from land caused the crew to want to turn back, Columbus was said to have read a verse, "Be of good cheer, It is I, Be not afraid." Math 14-27 And he may have added Isaiah 35 verse 4, " Say to them that are of fearful heart, Be strong , fear not, behold your God will come with vengeance, even God with a recompense, He will save you." The seas became less rough a report noted.

Columbus is said to have written : " What I conceive to be the principle wish of our most sincere King, the conversion of those people to the Holy Faith of Christ." Although Christopher Columbus later in his life was discredited for not finding riches of gold and silver, he never lost his faith in the Lord. Columbus himself, saw his accomplishments differently than recorded in the history books we all studied in the classrooms. He met his primary goal of spreading the light to a lost world with the Christian religion, he told other believers of his time.

We can all be a missionary as we give the Good News to those around us. Pray this Sunday we will all be in the church of our choice singing and worshiping our Lord and Savior Jesus Christ.

God Bless America

Christian Fellowship

*I*t is a blessing to have Christian friends in our everyday life and those that we associate with daily. While we may have business relationships, friendly neighbors and relatives that we respect, there is something special about knowing they are also acquainted with our gracious and loving Lord Jesus Christ.

We see in the Bible where we are given instructions to walk with the Lord and with Christian companions, 1 John, Chapter 1, Verse 7, " But if we walk in the light, as He is the light, we have fellowship with one another, and the blood of Jesus Christ His Son cleanses us from all sin."

On Memorial Day, our church has a church picnic for a few hours in a local park, We get to have Christian Fellowship with long time church members, new members, Christians that may have been only visiting and others that are curious about what a Christian life is all about. It is a wonderful day to greet one another, watch the kids fly kites, and play games, bring our favorite dish to share, and cook on the charcoal embers a delightful meat item. I had for the first time , a very pleasing to taste and smell, cranberry hamburger with all the trimmings , given to me by a new church friend.

Christians are companions, that build on each other, as we study the Bible and prayer together. The trials and tribulations that we face as an individual seem so much smaller, if we look to our Lord Jesus Christ and His church for the answers to our problems.

Our Lord tells us in Hebrews, Chapter 13, Verse I and 2, " Let brotherly love continue. Do not forget to entertain strangers, for by doing some have unwittingly entertained angels". Yes, people visiting church and church picnics maybe strangers to us but they should be welcomed whole heartily with a warm and friendly greeting . That is Christian Fellowship.

Let us all join in singing and worshiping our Lord and Savior Jesus Christ in the church of our choice this coming Sunday.

God Bless America

Born Again

When the Lord blesses us with a new born child, we as the parents agree on a name and the birth is recorded in the official records. The local newspaper usually lists the wonderful event for all to view . Relatives, friends and neighbors congratulate us and want to see the newborn child and we are very proud parents.

As we go through life and our physical body is nourished with love and care by our parents as we grow to be a fine boy or girl. However, being raised in a Christian family and learning to love the Lord Jesus Christ in Sunday School and by attending church with our parents, we also see the positive life the Lord can give us.

As a child we may not have fully understood that we needed to have both a relationship with our parents and with our Lord Jesus Christ. We see in the Bible, 1 Corinthians, Chapter 13, Verse 11. " When as a child I spoke as a child, I understood as a child, I thought as a child, but when I became a man, I put away childish things".

At an accountable age for our actions, we decided to ask the Lord into our life and give our life over to Him as a Christian. When this happens it is like being born again a second time with a new spiritual body, as we want to serve our Lord and Savior Jesus Christ. We remember the time and place and it is recorded with a baptismal service soon after, as we announce to the world our new spiritual birth as a Christian.

We see in the Bible where Jesus is speaking to us in the Book of John Chapter 3, Verse 3, " Jesus answered and said, " Most assuredly I say to you, unless one is born again, he cannot see the kingdom of God".

As we pray and worship the Lord, each day we grow from a newborn Christian to where we are in our stage of Christian growth today. As we grow in faith, we find ourselves bubbling over with the joy the Lord provides and we want to share the Gospel with those we come in contact.

No matter what our background or our condition today, we can experience the second birth by asking the Lord Jesus Christ to come into our life and repent of our sin. Yes, the Lord is there to reach His hand out to us and carry us over the trails and tribulations we face each day, as He puts us under His care on the solid higher ground . We are all sinners saved by His grace, and He offers it to us freely.

As we age, we realize that no matter how much we exercise, eat the right foods, and protect our physical body, someday we will lay it in the grave. Our spiritual body, however if we put our Hope, Trust and Faith in the Lord Jesus Christ, will live on for eternity as He takes us home to be with Him,

Trust this Sunday we will all be in the church of our choice singing and worshiping the Lord.

God Bless America

God's Blessings

Nature is all around us in everything we do, however, we may not see the wonderful creations our loving Lord has provided. Living on a farm most of my life, it is a blessing to be so close to the creatures God has made available to us for our benefit.

Recently we had four calves born within the period of a few weeks. The mother cow removed herself from the cow herd to give birth to her calf. In only a matter of a less than a hour the young newborn calf is up and nursing from it's loving mother. She shows her love as she cleans the new baby calf and teaches it to obey her commands.

Today the baby heifer calf is three days old and the mother calls it to come to her. The baby with out delay responds promptly to it's mothers call. The other calves, at times also respond and soon the mother cow is baby sitting all the calves for an hour or two. I hand feed the mother cow through the fence a treat of alfalfa cubes which are like giving candy bars to our children.

As the calves wait, a pair of quail came to investigate the happenings in the pasture. These birds are so tame and seem not to be afraid of the calves or me, as I feed the cow. They jump up on the fence panel just a few feet away and continue to observe and watch us.

This reminds me of the Lord coming into our life and we become a new born Christian. As we put our trust and faith in His loving care, we gain strength and begin praying and reading the Bible. We see in the Bible in the Book of 1 Peter, 1Chapter 2, Verses 2and 3, " As newborn babes, desire the pure milk of the word, that you may grow thereby. if indeed you have tasted that the Lord is gracious.

When the church bells beckon us to worship at the church we chose, we are joined by other believers to sing and worship our Lord and Savior Jesus Christ. After hearing the message from the Lord , we are instructed in the Bible to share with others the Word Of God. As we bubble over with the Lord's love, those we come in contact, can see a happy Christian . The Bible tells us, Colossians Chapter 3, Verse 16, ' Let the Word of Christ dwell in you richly in all wisdom. teaching and admonishing one another in psalms and hymns and spiritual songs, singing with grace in your hearts to the Lord".

There may be those that are sitting on the fence and just curious about the way of life of a Christian, Then, other people may be just waiting for us to welcome them to join us in church and experience a true loving spiritual life that only the Lord and Savior Jesus Christ can provide. Let us spread the gospel though out the land as we serve our most gracious Lord who first loved us.

Trust we will all be in the church of our choice this Sunday singing and worshiping our Lord Jesus Christ.

God Bless America

What Goes Around Comes Around

Over the years of our youth we may do things that seem not important, however, in later years they maybe a wonderful memory. If we take the time to help our neighbors, friends, classmates, and those we come in contact with, we see a verse in the Bible that gives us instructions. Our Lord Jesus Christ is telling us in the Book of John, Chapter 15, Verse 17, " These things I command you, that you love one another."

When I was a teenager in Iowa, so many years ago, I had a daily newspaper route while in Jr and High School. Through all kinds of weather the paper was delivered by bicycle in the summer and pulling a sled in the cold and snow of winter. With over a hundred newspapers the Sunday morning delivery was especially difficult after a winter snowstorm when the walkways had not been cleared. Half way through the delivery route I could most always count on a kind Greek lady having a cup of hot chocolate waiting for me when I placed her paper in the door.

This lady would tell me how they appreciated the American way of life and they attended church every Sunday. She knew when I was running late and would say, "Hurry you will be late for your church". On the holidays of Easter and Christmas, this kind lady would bake a special cake with a whole egg in the center of it, and send it home with me for my family. I enjoyed hearing about Greece but never dreamed I would ever live there. However, that all changed when the Air Force sent me to the Support Group stationed at the Athens Airport.

While in Greece my wife and I would enjoy going into the remote countryside and a Greek fellow employee would go with us to help with the language and show us the sights. At one small out of way restaurant, we stopped to eat and enjoy the beautiful Mediterranean Sea view of the calm waters. The fish dinner was nice but my wife wanted the fish head removed and we all enjoyed the outstanding Greek meal and dessert.

At the next table, I heard a man speaking English and he mentioned Iowa where he lived in the United States. I asked him, what part of Iowa and he said the northeast section, town of Waterloo. As I looked at him, he seemed familiar, and when he mentioned living on West 7th Street, by the high school, I said I carried a newspaper route there for several years. I then recalled the kindness of the Greek lady, and told him how she would treat me so well. After his wife went home to be with the Lord, he retired from John Deere Tractor Co. and had recently returned to Greece to be with his extended family. The chance of us meeting in such a distant location has always been a Blessing from the Lord.

We read in the Bible, 1 Timothy, Chapter 4, Verse 12, " Let no man despise the youth, but be an example of the believers, in word, in conversation, in charity, in spirit, in faith, and in purity". Things we do as a youth help mold us and as we grow in the Christian life we should try to pass those good building blocks to others we come in contact .

Pray we will all be in the church of our choice on Sunday, singing and worshiping our Savior and Lord Jesus Christ who loves us and is always there to guide us.

God Bless America

Evil For Evil

*A*s we attend church over our lifetime, there are some sermons that the Lord sends us that really get our attention. Often we can relate our own personal experiences to the message and see where we may have been guilty of not doing the Christian way as the Bible tells us.

We see in Romans Chapter 12, Verse 17, " Recompense to no man evil for evil, Provide things honest in the sight of all men." \

I am sure we all can recall a time when we said, "I will get even for that unjust thing which was done to me". Do we get even, which we think at the time will make us feel better, or do we turn the other cheek as the Bible tells us?

We are told in Verse 18 and 19, " It be possible, as much as lieth in you , live peaceably with all men, Dearly beloved, do not avenge yourselves, but rather give place unto wrath: for it is written, "Vengeance is mine. I will repay," saith the Lord."

I remember a time when I was really upset. I operated a Texaco Service Station and Ryder Truck Rental in Marysville, CA and while gasoline then was only 25 cents a gallon, it really bothered me that thieves were stealing gas from the rental trucks. So one night I parked a block away and waited to see who was taking the gasoline. When a car drove into the lot and gas was being taken from a large tank the trucks had, I called the police and they responded. The thief was caught red handed and I told the officer if he wants the gas so bad I will dump it in the backseat of his car. I was quickly informed I would be arrested for destroying property, so calmed down and asked if I could speak with the man detained in the police car?

He told me that earlier that day he had been released from California Medical Facility, a state prison in Vacaville, CA about 60 miles away and was on the way to his sisters in Reno, Nevada. She had obtained a car for him but it had little gas to make the trip and saw the Ryder Trucks as a source. I told the police officer, I wanted to put the 5 gallons of gas in his fuel tank and send him on his way. The officer said you are not going to file charges? I said no he needs a friend right now, and just maybe he will change his lifestyle, so send him to his sister in Reno. For a little over a dollar, I became a friend in his time of need., and also had a good feeling as he drove away.

Our Lord tells us in Verse20, "Therefore: "If your enemy is hungry, feed him; If he is thirsty, give him a drink; For in so doing you will bring coals of fire on his head." And Verse 21, " Do not be overcome by evil, but overcome evil with good.

Trust this Sunday we will all be in the church of our choice singing and worshiping our loving Savior and Lord Jesus Christ.

God Bless America

Seven Pillars Of a Great Marriage

Recently my pastor gave an evening sermon on the seven pillars of a great marriage. Since I am a widower, sort of figured they might apply if I ever entered that adventure area again, so I had better take some notes. So here are my thoughts as a writer on the oldest institution the Bible mentions.

> 1. Marriage is a covenant not a contract as we normally think when we tie the knot. A contract is time limiting, as if we buy a car or a 30 year house mortgage, and often comes with a guarantee, like the 20 year lifetime roof on our home. However, we find Marriage is a covenant, all encompassing to include, in rich and poorer, in health and sickness, till death due us part. That covers a lot of circumstances and my covenant lasted for 55 years till the Lord called my wife home.

> 2. Marriage is not a 50 yard dash where we go full steam ahead for a short period of time and give it our all. Marriage is a marathon and we are in it for the long haul as we work together to reach our goal of living a Christian life together.

> 3. Marriage is an investment and just maybe the most demanding of our time and energy. It succeeds if we give it love, charity and forgiveness. Like all longtime

investments we cannot take out more than we put in, if we want our investment to grow.

4. Marriage is a learning experience and from time to time needs adjustments. Like the days of the horse and buggy, we now have faster means of travel with our automobile. Many workers had to make adjustments or fall behind and marriage is in constant adjustment as we seek to please our LORD and partner.

5. Marriage is serving everyday with a desire to please our spouse and have a loving relationship. It is better to give true love and service and be happy, then to expect to receive with out giving of ourselves.

6. Marriage is spiritual and not a combat zone. When we were married, do you recall the groom is at the alter waiting to receive his bride. She is so beautiful as she come down the isle to become a partner with the one she loves in a scriptural union. We soon feed each other wedding cake and it is a continual blessing to share our lives with each other, We sign an official document recording our covenant with each other and ask the Lord for his blessing as we head off into the unknown together.

7. Now the most important part of a Marriage is to put our Gracious and Loving Lord Jesus Christ first in our lives. As we share our prayers with each other, read the Bible together, and attend the church of our choice, we grow spiritually in our relationship with our Lord and it also strengthens our marriage that we have just committed to here on earth.

Trust we will all be in the church of our choice singing and praising in worship our Lord and Savior Jesus Christ this Sunday.

God Bless America

Church Family

When we think of family, we have all different ideas of just what it takes to make the ideal Christian family. Some of us have large families with many children and then we expanded from there to give us numerous relatives. At a family gathering my immediate relatives were in excess of forty and we all share in the blessings and times of trial that each of us face. Other families are much smaller but the bond is very strong between family members as they enjoy the companionship the family provides.

As a church member, we also belong to a family of believers that pray and uphold each other, as we join in the worship of our gracious and loving Lord and Savior Jesus Christ. We are blessed with our pastor as he heads up our church family and gives us the truth as the Lord leads and speaks to him.

Recently, we had a Family Church Camp at a beautiful lake about 70 miles up in the mountains. It is noted for the scenery and blue waters that provide excellent fishing, swimming and boating. The camp store known all over the area for the large ice cream selection and monstrous ice cream cones is a hit with all the church family. Church members get an opportunity to cook in the open and share their wonderful creations of tempting, tasty, and delicious food items with all the family. One man is famous for his clam chowder, a lady makes spaghetti and Italian sausage which is a hit with the kids, and others provide interesting salads and deserts.

We see in the Bible where church family camps are not new " Exodus 10-9. " And Moses said, We will go with our young and with our old, with our sons and with our daughters, with our flocks and with our herds will we go, for we must hold a feast until the Lord."

We sometime invite family and friends to the Family Church Camp as our guests . There we all enjoy the activities, great food, and evening services of singing, with a Bible test given to us as a challenge. and prayer. I invited my daughter and she joined us at the camp with grand children and great grand children of all ages. However, her husband who is retired, did not come as he felt he had more important things to do at the ranch/farm. On the second day he was working with a wrench and it slipped and knocked out some front teeth and he ran to the house. In the process the farm gate was left open and the animals escaped, the sheep , the goats and two large emus. They, seeing their freedom, headed for the highway as an escape route. He managed to get the animals rounded up and back in the pasture but it was some experience. He called his wife just before the evening service; my daughter said if he had been at the Church Family Camp, where her husband belonged, this would not have happened, We as a church family prayed for his quick recovery in the evening prayer service, as that may have been the Lord's way of speaking to my son in law.

The church family is very important to Christian men and women as we grow and mature in the Christian faith just as we do in our family group. Well the family church camp came to an end and we each headed to our homes, all rested and energized to praise and worship the Lord.

We pray on Sunday, we are all at the church of our choice worshiping our Lord and Savior Jesus Christ.

God Bless America

Vacation Bible School

*A*s we go through the summer season each year, the Christian community looks forward to reaching out to children of our area with Vacation Bible Schools. Our country church had one this past week It takes a church effort of prayer, service and dedication to coordinate the extensive planning with some twenty five teachers and counselors involved.

We see in the Bible, Proverbs Chapter 22, Verse 6, " Train up a child in the way he should go, and when he is old he will not depart from it."

The young children ages 5 to 12 are full of energy and eager to learn about our Lord and Savior Jesus Christ. Activities of crafts, outdoor games, puppet shows, and youth video Christian songs displayed on large sound screens all go into the Vacation Bible School program of learning. We also had a competition between age groups on Red and Blue teams and as the week progressed each child was dedicated to having their team be the winner.

On the first night 29 children attended and enjoyed the activities and on the second night they invited their friends so the total attendance had reached 51 excited bubbling over children. I invited four of my granddaughters from out of the area to come stay on the farm and attend Vacation Bible School.

The granddaughters love to visit, feed the chickens, talk to the cows, and help in the large church garden with watering and picking the vegetables. Early in the week the temperature became hot, hot, and hot reaching 104 degrees one day during midweek. I was asked, grandfather can you take us swimming? At my age I cannot stay in the sun and heat very long, so told them I knew of an indoor pool in a nearby town. They all got ready and we drove to the swimming pool all anxious to cool off from the intense heat. On arriving we noticed the temperature sign read 22 degrees and the pool was frozen over. They said grandpa you fooled us, this is an ice skating rink. They had never been on ice skates and after a few tumbles and falls they were up and quickly learn the skills of ice skating. We visited the frozen swimming pool three times during the week and grandpa felt like a kid again. We also volunteered as a cleaning crew at the church and I witnessed the young girls expertise with vacuum cleaners as they made the Vacation Bible School areas sparkle.

It was a real blessing during the week to see three of my granddaughters ask Jesus to come into their hearts and witness on Friday a total of eight children baptized into the Christian family. My other granddaughter was saved at the Bible Camp held at a mountain retreat last year. They want to come back next year and attend Vacation Bible School it was so much fun. Grandpa felt not like an old eighty but more like a young 40 year old for a wonderful enjoyable week.

Trust this Sunday we will all be at the church of our choice singing and worshiping our Lord and Savior Jesus Christ.

God Bless America

Left Handed Blessing?

As I have gone through life, have often wondered why I was born left handed? Recently saw a report stated that only 7% of the world population is born left handed. Now that is a very small minority that I find myself, so this got me to wondering. why is everything for the right handed person?

We see most baseball players batting right handed and the cars at intersections approaching from the right have the right away. We can make a right hand turn on a red light, and even the correct answers to tests and contests are called right answer. Then when a person is sworn into an office they place their right hand on the Bible. When we enter a store with two doors the right hand one is inbound and on leaving we exit by way of the right hand door. Even in nature we see water flushed has a right hand spiral, as it goes down the drain.

I thought maybe the Bible would help me in searching for an answer. Is God right or left handed as he says His Son Jesus Christ will be seated at His right hand? We see in the Old Testament, Psalms 110-1, " The Lord said to my Lord, Sit at my right hand, till I make your enemies your footstool." Then in Isaiah, 41, verse 10, " Fear not, for I am with thee, be not dismayed, for I am thy God. I will strengthen thee, yea,, I will help you, I will uphold thee with my righteous right hand."

In the New Testament, we see our Lord and Savior Jesus Christ speaking. Matthew, Chapter 23, verses 33 and 34, " And he will sit the sheep on

His right hand, but the goats on His left." The King will say to those on His right hand, " Come you Blessed of my Father in trust the Kingdom prepared for you from the foundation of the earth." In Revelation, 2-2, we see." These things He who holds the seven stars in his right hand, who walks in midst of the seven golden lamp stands."

However, Apostle Paul, says in 1 Corinthians,. Chapter 7,Verse7. " For I wish that all men were even as I myself. But each one has his own gift from God, one in his manner and another in that".

At this point I was at a loss to find why God created left handed people, so asked my Pastor, Gerald Harder for his help. He said the Bible, however does mention lefties. And they are most up lifting verses.

Proverbs 3:16 " Length of day is in her right hand, and in her left hand riches and honor." Also in Judges 20-16 , "Among all this people there were seven hundred chosen men left handed, every one could sling stones at an hair breadth, and not miss." Pastor add, " Would hate to get in an argument with these guys".

Yes, each of us have a gift from God whether we are right handed or left handed. Our God sent His Son our Gracious Lord and Savior Jesus Christ to die on the cross and give us an avenue to God . We read in John 3 , verses 16 and 17, " For God so loved the world that He gave His only begotten Son, that whoever believes in Him should not perish but have everlasting life. "For God did not send His Son into the world to condemn the world, but that the world through Him might be saved."

As a left handed person we may not get all the benefits granted the majority of right handed people, however our Lord makes no distinction. We all are offered His love and salvation, if we only ask Him into our hearts. Yes, let us put our Hope, Trust and Faith in our Lord and Savior Jesus Christ.

Pray each of us will be in the church of our choice on Sunday, signing and worshipping , no matter if we hold the song book in different hands.

God Bless America

Wonderful Day Every Day

Our loving and gracious Lord Jesus Christ has provided us with a life filled with wonderful days of all kinds. We are told to praise Him according to God's Word, the Bible, for everything that comes our way.

In Psalm 71, verses 5 and 6 we read, " For You are my Hope, O Lord God; You are my trust from youth. By You I have been upheld from birth; You are He that took me out of my mother's womb. My praise shall be continually to You".

When we see one of our Christian friends go home to be with the Lord, we should offer praise to our glorious Savior. When our Lord calls home our sister or brother we may for a time grieve the loss. In our Bible, Matthew Chapter 5, Verse 5, " Blessed are those that morn, For they shall be comforted".

However, funerals should be a time of rejoicing , for our Lord has assured us with his words of comfort; "To be absent from of the body is to be home with the Lord". He says in John 14 verse 2, " In my Father's house are many mansions, if it were not so I would have told you. I go to prepare a place for you".

Recently, my younger brother, to everyone's surprise was called home by the Lord. He was an athletic type person in high school and college and a Christian business man that the Lord blessed over and over. He and his wife traveled the world, as they walked on the Wall of China, visited the home of our president in Africa, and stood on the place where Apostle Paul spoke to the Athenians in Athens. Greece. He never forgot his humble beginning as an Iowa country boy and shared and helped all those he came in contact. My brother's life was of continually praising and worshiping the Lord, however, we do not know the Lord's plans for our life, as we try to walk in His footsteps.

We will no matter how well we treat our physical body, even with the proper nourishment , proper exercise and protection from the elements and dangers, someday lay our body in the grave. Our Lord and Savior Jesus Christ, if we put our Hope, Faith and Trust in Him and repent of our sins, has assured us He will take us home with Him and give us eternal life. It is not the few years given us here on earth, with all the trials and tribulations that we encounter , but a life in heaven, a place where there is only wonderful days every day for ever.

Trust, we all be in the church of our choice this Sunday as we join with other Christians in the singing and worshiping of our Lord Jesus Christ.

God Bless America

Bridge Builder

When we think of all the bridges built in the history of the world, those constructed by the Roman Empire in Biblical times have stood the test of time. The bridge in Adana, Turkey, that still stands today with heavy traffic use, was walked upon by Apostle Paul on his journeys from his home Tarsus just 20 miles away. I was privileged to cross it many times while living in Turkey. It was built before the birth of our Lord and still carries heavy trucks and cars with two lanes each way.

Another bridge we all recognize is the London Bridge, a bridge that was a marvel in its time. As a kid we all played London Bridge Is Falling Down which likewise is a game that is now history. Another outstanding magnificent bridge that all the world knows well is the Golden Gate Bridge. It stands as a beacon of hope to the world and the western gateway to America. When growing up in Iowa as a country boy we visited the wooden covered bridges that are well known and we see in beautiful pictures. Most are no longer in use due to unsafe conditions of the wooden construction.

The greatest bridge builder of all time is our gracious and loving Lord and Savior Jesus Christ. He built a bridge to heaven from two pieces of wood and three nails. By His dying on the cross. we are given an avenue to a heavenly home with our Lord Jesus for eternity. We see in the Bible. Luke, Chapter 22 Verse34, Then Jesus said, " Father forgive them, for they do not know what they do." and our Lord adds in Verse46, And He said to them, "Thus it is written, and thus it is necessary for the Christ to suffer and to rise from the dead on the third day, and that repentance and remission of sins should be preached in His name to all nations, beginning at Jerusalem.

If we put our hope. trust, and faith in our Lord Jesus Christ and repent of our sins and are born again as a Christian, we can travel on the bridge to heaven our Lord has provided. It is not a bridge built by man that has structure weakness and becomes impassable with age. It is a heavenly bridge that the Lord uses to take us home when we die and leave our earthly body in the grave. To be absent of the body is to be home with our Lord Jesus Christ.

Trust each of us will be the church of our choice this Sunday worshiping our Lord and Savior Jesus Christ.

God Bless America

Happy Christian

One of this column readers sent me a list of 39 things that make for a happy Christian life that she had complied. I had never seen such a detailed listing of major and minor ways a Christian could use for a happy life. It got me to questioning my short list of ten or so things. They have kept me happy and also have carried me through the times when I drifted away from keeping my eyes on our Gracious and Loving Lord Jesus Christ. That is when I found myself a really unhappy Christian, in an unhappy state of mind, as I looked to myself for answers instead of looking up to the Lord.

We fully agreed on the the most important item to top the list.

> 1. — Prayer. That is the most powerful tool the Lord has given us as we see in the Bible Acts 6-4 " But we will our selves continually to prayer". Also our Lord tells us in Matthew 7 -7, Ask and it will be given to thee, seek and you will find, knock and it will opened to thee." Yes, no matter in what circumstances we may find ourselves, our Lord is there for us, if we only place our burden on Him to carry and seek his guidance.

> 2. — I have always closely tied Praise and giving thanks to the Lord for all His Blessings He has showered on us over our life as a Christian. In Psalm 71-8 we read,

" Let my mouth be filled with Your praise and with Your glory all the day." The more we praise the Lord for his answers to our prayers the more He wants to please us. We are His servant and we some times let our pride get in the way, thinking we accomplished this or that but we are nothing without the Lord leading us on the pathway of happiness.

3.— Go to bed on time, she tells me is vitally important. So I agree, the old saying for a farmer boy like me, has been. Early to bed and early to rise, makes a man healthy, wealthy and wise. Yes, a clear head is important, so we need our sleep. The Bible makes a point to us in Psalms 127-2 , " It is vain for you to rise up early and to sit up late, To eat the breads of sorrow, For so He gives His beloved sleep."

4. — Pace our selves- Do not take on more then we can accomplish and still do it in an outstanding manner. Have others be able to count on you to do a task, big or small, that you have agreed to perform. Be able to to say no if your time schedule is full, in a polite Christian way.

5. — Separate worries from concerns - It is a sin to worry but often we are concerned about something that effects us. Turn it over the Lord for His direction and have a good nights rest.

6 — K. M. S. (Keep Mouth Shut) This piece of advise can prevent an enormous amount of trouble. I have trouble with this as many do, so I need to learn to engage my brain before speaking.

7. — Do something for the kid in you everyday- Take time to smell the roses and enjoy the life God has given you. Work and no play makes for a dull life, so take a vacation from the daily schedule and enjoy all the wonderful things the Lord has provided .

8. — Having problems, talk to God on the spot. Remember, the shortest bridge between despair and hope is often a good—"Thank You Jesus".

9. Develop a forgiving attitude — Most people are doing the best they can and remember to be kind to the unkind people as they may need it the most.

10. — Every night before bed in prayers, think of something that you are grateful for that God has given you. The Lord showers His blessings on us as we try to walk at His side or in His footsteps. He is our friend like none other and has a way of turning things around for us. As the Bible tells us in Romans 8-31, " If God is for us, who can be against us."

Trust this Sunday we will all be in the church of our choice singing and worshiping our gracious and loving Lord and Savior Jesus Christ.

God Bless America

A Life Of Blessings

This column is a little different as it tells about the the life of this writer whom turned 80 years young this week. My children, grands, and greats gathered to give me a birthday party and they wanted a story about my life. Also as a new member of Toastmasters, this also became my first talk introducing my life. It has been an interesting time of adventure and travel which I was able to share with my wife before she went home.

I was not expected to live as a newborn baby, according to my mother. The doctors told her I had medical problems including a heart murmur and was not gaining weight as a normal baby. My parents prayed for the Lords help and He answered their prayers. So I was born on Sep 27, 1932, in the bad depression year. in Waterloo, Iowa. My full name is Leonard Allen Granger but go now by Len.

As a child I recall people asking my mother why don't you feed Len, he looks so pale and thin. During high school I played in the band and my brother was a standout football star . The girls wanted to go out on dates with me just to talk about my brother, so I had few dates.

After high school, I graduated from Gates Business College and worked at Rath Packing Co, training in management. Most of the co-workers were ex Army Air Force so I joined the AF and headed for California. Here I met my wife, a great dancer, at a USO high school dance, I was able to talk to her for about a half hour and told her I had gone to business college, and did not smoke, drink or dance. Then she asked if I would like to go home with her and meet her parents. What a surprise for a country pumpkin like me from Iowa, fast California gals.?

I never learned to dance, but we were engaged in 3 months and married at 6 months when she finished high school. I was 20 and she was 17 so our parents signed for us to get married I was a 1 strip GI and she was the daughter of the superintendent of the General Motors assembly plant in San Leandro, CA , so we had many adjustments in our life style. I learned to duck when cans of beans were thrown at me and that stopped when they went through a glass window. I was kicked out of bed and broke 2 ribs the second week of marriage. But I learned how to tame her down and we did our own dance having 6 children in our 55 years of marriage.

I stayed in the Air Force for 23 years and we traveled to all the states except AK and HI, serving at bases in many of them. Spent 4 years in Greece, with the 7206 Support Group, assigned to the Athens Airport and attached to the American Embassy . There the Lord protected me and took me off a flight out of Naples, Italy before it crashed and all on board were killed. I was also an OSI ,Office Of Special Investigations Agent mole, so was sent all over Europe and the states. My last assignment was at Beale AFB, CA and retired there in 1973. Graduated from Yuba College and soon had five businesses with 17 employees and two houses, In 1983, sold everything and moved back to the farm and home we built in 1960 while stationed at Travis AFB, CA.

I have always put my faith in Lord and He has blessed me over and over, Today I write a newspaper column for the local paper, called Lens Lines. Have been in the wholesale fishing tackle industry for past 43 years as a wagon jobber to stores and marinas. I try to give back from the farm the produce and meat from the beef cattle to help those in need .

Over the years, I have tried to do a little better than what my name initials indicate. It has taken me all my life, with help from above, to be were I am today. But I am still Leonard Allen Granger, yes it is L.A.G. when I print my initials.

Trust we will be in the church of our choice this Sunday, singing and worshiping our Lord and Savior Jesus Christ.

God Bless America

Yes, God Answers Prayers

Often when we pray to our Lord and Savior Jesus Christ we may think; Did He hear my prayer and how long will it be before I get answer? We are sometimes impatient and think just maybe I can solve my own problem after we asked the Lord for His help. Our gracious Lord has His own timetable and we as believers cannot rush the outcome. It maybe not what we want to hear when the answer comes to us but it is for our best interest, you can be assured.

In the Bible we read where the Lord tells us in Book of Matthew, Chapter 7 and Verse 7, " Ask, and it will be given to you, seek, and you will find, knock, and it will opened to you. Verse 8, adds " For everyone that asks receives, and he who seeks finds, and to him that knocks it will be given."

If we put our Hope, Trust, and Faith in our Lord Jesus Christ how can we go wrong as He is a Friend, Guide, and Comforter like none other we will ever know. I can relate often to answered prayer and the outcome is sometimes very much a cliff hanger.

When my wife went home to be with the Lord 4 years ago, the Lord sent me an angel to live on the farm and be my companion. I believe my wife and her widowed sister in law knew I would need help to operate a farm and live a Christian life on my own. So with the Lord's direction, I have been blessed over and over, and He also even opened the door to writing this column. We added the granddaughter, age 18 to our household and assisted her to attend medical college. However, she needed reliable transportation, so I bought and gave a nearly new car to my sister in law. which she loaned the granddaughter to make the daily trip to the out of town college.

After graduation she found work and still needed the auto to get back and forth to her place of employment and when she moved to a friend's house and then later to her boyfriends home she kept the automobile. In the meantime my sister in law paid all the high insurance, maintenance and license costs with little hope of ever seeing her car again. So we prayed for the Lord to give us an answer as my sister in law wants to return to her home in the near future and will need the car for transportation. Many prayers went out over several months but there seemed to be no answer as we waited and waited.

A couple days ago my sister in law got a phone call from her granddaughter telling her she had just totaled out the car in an accident; no one was injured. My sister in law was crying as she told me, she now had no car. I said please do not cry that is the Lord's answer to our prayers and you should be rejoicing. You may not have that car, but you no longer have any high insurance to pay, tires to replace, license to renew, and the insurance will send you a check for its value. In a matter of minutes she went from tears to smiles as she realized, Yes. The Lord answers prayers.

Trust this Sunday, we will all be in the church of our choice singing and praising our Gracious and Loving Lord Jesus Christ who answers our prayers.

God Bless America

Atheist Way Of Life

The Lord tells us in the Bible to spread the Good Word to all we may come in contact. Sometimes we see individuals that promote their lifestyle of denying there is a God . They are very bold in expressing the goal of what they believe is right for everyone. We see highway billboards across the country stating in various statements about how we no longer need God in our lives.

The other day I was waiting in a checkout line at the grocery store and a young man in his 20's. behind me had on a tee shirt with the following statement. "Thank God I Am An Atheist". I spoke to him that his message sort of confused me. He was saying there is a God and he had thanked Him, so he agreed there is a God. Then in the next few words he says he is an Atheist that does not believe there is a God. The young man was not very talkative but he said I am an Atheist. I wondered why he mentioned God and did not just say "I am an Atheist"? Seems he is sort of confused and did not want to offend God, as he thanked Him.

We see in the Bible: Psalm 14: 1-5 " The fool hath said in his heart, There is no God. They are corrupt, they have done abominable works, there is none that doeth good. The LORD looked down from heaven upon the children of men, to see if there was any that did not understand, and seek God. They are all gone aside, they are all together become filthy, there is none that doeth good, no, not one—."

The wonderful blessings the Lord has provided all of us are everywhere for our viewing and enjoyment. It is hard to believe there is not a higher being as we cannot change anything on our own, and are at the Lord's mercy . We see in the Bible, where the Lord speaks to us, Matthew. Chapter 10, verse 33—" For whomever denies me before men, him I will also deny before my Father who is in heaven."

I feel sorry for the Atheist, especially the young people that feel they are in charge of all things and they can control their lives and an make it a life to their pleasing without the Lord's direction. When the trials and tribulations come their way in later life, in the form of health problems that even challenge the doctors, financial failures or economic loss of maybe a source of employment. or problems that may result in depression in their lives that may effect their mind and thinking, where will they turn for answers?

Will the Atheist realize, there is a higher power that causes the sun to shine each day. the earth to provide us food, fuel and shelter and many other things for our needs? We may give our bodies the best of the foods , go to the gym for exercise, drive a safe automobile, and educate our minds, but we all will lay our bodies in the grave at some point in time. Only if we have put our Hope, Trust, and Faith in our gracious and loving Lord and Savior Jesus Christ do we have a place in heaven. The Bible tells us to be absent from the body is to home with the Lord.

Trust this Sunday we will all be the church of our choice singing and worshiping our Lord and Savior Jesus Christ,

God Bless America

A Half Christian

Several years ago my wife wanted a new radio sound system in our station wagon, so we went to a chain store. We waited patiently while the system was installed The new speakers mounted on the car dash were replaced to give us all around sound.

When I went to pick up the auto, I noticed the right side of the windshield had a large crack from top to the bottom. The manager said, yes they accidentally broke it when using an installation tool. However, they only broke half the window, so will only pay for half of the replacement costs. I was surprised with their thinking and said the windshield is either broken or not broken, there is no half way. I had to sign a release form in order to get may vehicle and got payment for half a window.

On arriving home, I called the companies main office in Los Angeles and talked with the PR representative, expressing my displeasure. He said he could not believe the managers decision and was embarrassed, Then he asked if she was a woman and I answered, Yes. He said now I understand the problem and will have the balance of the replacement money in the mail today, adding there is no such thing as a half a broken windshield.

There was a time in my life I felt like a half a Christian. I was raised in a church family as my mother played the piano in our church, I was at all the services when ever the doors were opened. Everyone thought I was saved, but I knew different. So at age twelve, I went forward in church and asked the Lord to become my Lord and Savior and was baptized giving notice to the world that I was a follower of our Gracious and Loving Lord Jesus Christ.

Just because we were dedicated to the Lord as a baby or baptized as a baby and have attended church all our lives, does not save us. We must ask the Lord to become our Savior on a particular time and place. We see in the Bible, John 3 -16, "For God so loved the world, that he gave his only begotten Son , that whosoever believeth in Him, should not perish, but have everlasting life". Then we see in John 14-6 when Jesus tells us, " I am the way, the truth, and the life, no man come to the Father , but by me. It was a great feeling knowing I had accepted the Lord and no longer felt like a half of a Christian. Now I felt like a shinny new windshield with a clear view , and could go out and spread the Good News to all those I came in contact.

Pray we will all be the church of our choice this Sunday, singing and worshiping our Lord and Savior Jesus Christ.

God Bless America

The Bridge To Nowhere.

Our gracious and loving Lord and Savior built a bridge to His Father and Heaven when He died on the rugged cross and shed His blood for us lost sinners. Untold numbers have become Christian believers since that day over 2,000 years ago, when our Lord died, was buried , and rose again on the third day. We have our living Lord sitting at the right hand of His Father, as He gives guidance and answers our prayers. He on leaving this world even thought of our well being as He left us a Comforter, the Holy Spirit until our Lord returns. Not all bridges in the time since the Lord built His have been so well traveled.

Let me tell you about the bridge to no where. It is built in Michigan's Paul Bunyan Country, the Upper Peninsula. It is a mythical land and one of the modern myths of today.

It was believed that a bridge linking the 2 peninsulas , the Upper, where I lived, and the Lower, a very prosperous area of our country including Detroit, the world capital of auto manufacturing in those days would do wonders. Many thought it would bring an enormous increase in tourist and instant prosperity to this frozen land. It is noted for an average 211 inches of snow and 70 below temps in the winter, but we also had some of the largest and best fishing found anywhere.

Jobs would abound with the bridge construction, but the Lower Penn was not very supportive. While the UP people are very nice, and the scenery is beautiful, the general feeling was it would be more economical to give the UP to Wisconsin, where it geographically belongs. At first large of sums of state tax funds poured into the northern area during the construction period and income and taxes from tourist boomed. However, in 1964 a study was made by the U.S. Department of Commerce, which surprised everyone. The Big Mackinac Bridge opened in 1957 and had produced tourist income in many millions but by 1966 when I was living there, it had lost the tourist interest and had income of less than half.

So then the people of the UP wanted the bridge to be toll free and devoting all gasoline tax dollars to reducing the bridge bonds. The state senate and people of Lower Peninsula, said a deal is a deal, "Give Us Bridge" and the tolls will pay for it.

We see where our Lord offers to take our spiritual body over His bridge to Heaven when we leave our physical body in the grave. There is no toll fee to pay, if we only put our Hope, Trust, and Faith in Him and repent of our sins. Our Lord's promise of eternal life with Him takes our man made decision to make a decision to ask the Lord as our Savior. He is the best friend we will ever know and He has the bridge to connect two peninsulas, earth and heaven for ever.

May we all join together in church of our choice this Sunday and worship our Lord and Savior Jesus Christ.

God Bless America

God's Creations

When I look around about me I see that God, the Master of the Universe, has created some wonders that we can only marvel at their existence. He has made not one tree but hundreds of different types from the sage of the deserts to the high towering redwood trees. Some are flowering and others produce fruit of all kinds that vary according to the area of the world we reside.

He gave us scenery that is fantastic, all the beautiful valleys and the mountains reaching into the clouds with rock formations of all colors to delight us. Ever climbed a mountain and looked at all the views it offers. I thank God for the wonderful eyes He gave us to see His creations.

God made hundreds of different animals to fill the earth. Great numbers remain as wild animals in the forest but for man he gave us, cattle, sheep, and swine to supply us a food supply. Then God gave us camels, horses and other animals to provide us transportation.

The vast oceans cover the major part of the earth and our gracious God has filled them with fish of all kinds. He even stocked the lakes for us land lovers that get sea sick, as the Lord has thought of every detail. We find fish of all types and they take different items of fishing tackle to catch the trophy ones, according to the waters we are fishing. The Lord has blessed me over and over again in the 43 years of serving the fishing tackle industry. I give praise to the Lord daily for His protection and the ability to still use my hands in preparing tackle items for delivery as a wagon jobber.

Our Lord even had a bit of humor when He filled the earth with his marvelous creations. A long necked giraffe animal, a long trunk elephant animal, others with long tails or beaks , He filled the oceans with fish some with chainsaw noses, and some not desirable for man's food supply but required to balance the ocean.

Then God made man to worship Him we see in Bible verse: Genesis 1-27" So God created man in His own image, in the image of God created he him, male and female created he them" They were to worship the Lord and serve Him, however, man has rebelled often and still does every day. Today we see our country has now turned away from God and less than 50% of the population believe there is a God that made all the wonderful things in the universe. No one but God could create the marvelous things He has made, so I pray we see our country returning to the God believing nation our forefathers established.

Let us all attend the church of our choice this Sunday and sing and worship our Lord and Savior Jesus Christ.

God Bless America

We Are Protected

As we go about our daily lives we see things happening all around us that often are evil and destructive. But our Lord has said in the Bible - Psalm 145 Verses 17 to 20. " The Lord is righteous in all His ways; The Lord is near to all that call upon Him, To all that call upon Him is truth; He will fill the desire of those who fear Him, He will also hear their cry and save them; The Lord preserves all that love Him, But all the wicked He will destroy ."

In our world of trials and temptation we can look to the Lord for all our answers, if we only put our Hope, Trust, and Faith in our gracious and loving Lord and Savior Jesus Christ. It is also most important that we have protection here on earth which is given us by our government at all levels; Nationally by our Armed Forces and locally by our police departments. As they protect us we pray that they look to the Lord for His guidance. However, we still have the right to bear arms, as our police cannot be everywhere, so we should also be wise as a serpent —and harmless as doves.

Recently, I was looking in some of the old fishing tackle boxes I had collected over the years. As a tackle store owner, widows would bring in fishing tackle that had been in storage for years and I would buy it or trade for fishing gear they wanted to give a relative. In one green metal tackle box I discovered a set of brass knuckles, often used to fight with hands, that must have been from the 1940's era. Wow, they are illegal to have in my possession, so my first thought was I will take them to our police department and turn them in. I had seen our Police Chief of Dixon, visiting different churches when I was delivering garden produce from our Church Garden , to local churches. I hoped he would not arrest me for having possession of the brass knuckles.

So I hastily made a trip to the Police Department and gave them to the Christian police chief as I did not want them to fall into the wrong hands. He thanked me and we talked about the history of the brass knuckles, and that he seen them years ago as a police officer, but the new officers had not; so would put them on display. I told him, I felt much better having delivered them and appreciated having a caring compassionate Christian Police Chief. Our Police chief is a prayer warrior in every way and he asked if we could pray before I left? It was a blessing as we prayed and thanked the Lord for the many Physical, Material, and Spiritual Blessings He gives us daily. Yes, the Lord is there to protect us and He guides our local authorities who look to Him for guidance.

Trust this Sunday we will all be in the church of our choice, singing and worshiping our Lord and Savior Jesus Christ.

God Bless America

The Lord Forgives Us

When we ask our gracious and loving Lord and Savior to come into our lives; He will gladly accept us no matter what condition we find ourselves. All we are required to do is make a sincere decision to accept the Lord as our Savior and repent of our sins. He will take away our sins and carry the burdens we have so long endured. Love, Joy and Peace comes into our heart and we become the happy Christian, that God intended us to be. It is sometimes hard to believe, we have a Lord that takes all the sins from us as we become His servant and put our Hope, Trust and Faith in Him. Since we are still prone to sin, we pray each day to the Lord for forgiveness as we see in the Bible: Romans 12- Verse12- " Rejoicing in Hope, patient in tribulation, continually steadfastly in prayer."

When I was attending Business College in 1951 during the simmer vacation I was hoping to find a summer job. One of the girl students at the college said her town, LaPorte City , Iowa about 30 miles away , was hiring at the Green Giant Canning company. If I got a job there her parents had a spare bedroom for rent. I applied and was accepted to a job that was going to be a real challenge, but I like new experiences. It was one of the most demanding jobs at the canning facility, the timer and cooker who operated the large steam cookers . These units numbering ten were arranged in a circle and I was located in pit at the base as I applied steam and then vented after the required time for the cooking. Up top was a crew of 6 men who would open and close the lids, lower the 240 cans into and out of each cooker , and secure the lockdowns. The only problem was the men on top were all from Jamaica and could not speak English, so we developed hand signals that seemed to work.

After the canned cream style corn was cooled and labeled the cases were stored in an enormous warehouse holding thousands of cases all on pallets. About 3 weeks before the end of the canning season , workers in the warehouse said they could hear cans exploding somewhere in the middle of the warehouse. They climbed around the top of the cases and located a pallet that had the exploding cans. With much effort they were able to bring that group of 10 cases outside and put on a bonfire to destroy them. I watched as the cans exploded high into the air and I accepted full responsibility for my error in the proper cooking of this series of cases.

That day I was called into the company office and fully expected the worse. I feared that I would be fired on the spot and discharged as I was the cause of this expensive mistake. To my surprise the management started telling me how all this long canning season I had never missed a day from work and the canning was always on schedule. In past years, many problems had occurred, but this was one of the best seasons ever due to my dedication and performance.

Then they mentioned the cans that were not cooked properly and said it was all their fault. They had made a big mistake bringing in cheap labor to work on my crew. How I had to use hand signals because of the language differences and it had worked almost 100% of the time. I could just feel how they were taking the blame from me and my mistakes. I was so relaxed as they shook my hand and I went back to doing my job.

We see how our Lord who died on the cross, shed His blood for us, was buried and rose again on the third day. likewise has taken all our sins on Him. . We in our lives made those sins , However, He our Lord has taken the burden from us, and we are a new person in Him.

Trust this Sunday each of us will be in the Church of our choice singing and worshiping our Lord and Savior Jesus Christ.

God Bless America

LENS LINES is now found on the Friday edition Religious Page of the Dixon Tribune, Dixon, California. USA,

The purpose of the column is to reach out to Christians of all denominations and others looking to unit with God's people in our local churches. Our churches are not all a like in the way they worship the Lord so we invite you to visit them and make a decision to attend the church of your choice. We pray we will see you in church Sunday.

In addition to our local newspaper column, Lens Lines had been accepted by several worldwide websites that help spread the Good Word to the far reaches of the world. We are like a missaionary but on the computer and praise the Lord for opening the doors to Len's Lines.

I want to thank the Lord who often furnishes me with subject matter during prayers at night, the readers who suggest subjects for columns, and Pastor Gerald Harder who kindly reviews Len's Lines.

Len's Lines is Christian first and you the reader, with the Lord's guidance, hopefully will attend the church of your choice and have a personal relationship with our most loving and gracious Lord and Savour Jesus Christ.